...for the highest... ...never know for sure whether...

...bring you yet and taking a chance. But, as...

...several days. In fact, this author can think of no... ...that...

...following on the next big social event which is bound to stir up some news...

...that the Duke and Duchess of Hastings have yet to entertain callers...

...And who could be surprised if their diligent efforts are rewarded with a...

...and emerged victorious with their prize. We shall wait and see what the futu...

...doors to the world. Scandalous Sketches. I believe that most of you must...

...know Mr. Phillipford has been a semi-permanent member of this town for...

...his next upcoming project. However, this time it is apparent that he has foun...

...as ever seen him stay in the town for as long as she can remember and there...

...all know, a muse only lasts until inspiration for the next exhibition is needed...

...caught up in all sorts of trouble and all for a few months of excitement and a...

...bition, you will have come to notice that a large number of the artist's works ha...

...conscience, however there is a certain lady who, I believe, has not yet attended...

...ings and someone spots the striking resemblance between the two. Of course th...

...nyway, what we do know is that a certain Mrs. Foxfield is taking a trip to...

...Mrs. Rutheford. Unless, that is, she has already seen it...?

INSIDE
BRIDGERTON

INSIDE
BRIDGERTON

SHONDA RHIMES AND BETSY BEERS

MARYSUE
RUCCI
BOOKS

SCRIBNER

NEW YORK LONDON TORONTO SYDNEY NEW DELHI

ACKNOWLEDGMENTS

We would like to acknowledge the cast, crew, writers, and creatives who have shared their experiences of bringing this show to life. Through generously giving time to complete interviews for both "Bridgerton: The Official Podcast" along with speaking with us directly, the Bridgerton family has provided authentic and colorful insight into how much work they've put into this show.

We would also like to thank Sandie Bailey, Elise Loehnen, Jennifer Joel, and Marysue Rucci, without whom this book would not have been possible.

CAST OF CHARACTERS YOU'LL HEAR FROM:

Betsy Beers & Shonda Rhimes

Chris Van Dusen, Creator

CAST

Adjoa Andoh, Lady Danbury

Julie Andrews, Lady Whistledown

Simone Ashley, Kate Sharma

Jonathan Bailey, Anthony Bridgerton

Sabrina Bartlett, Siena Rosso

Harriet Cains, Phillipa Featherington

Bessie Carter, Prudence Featherington

Charithra Chandran, Edwina Sharma

Nicola Coughlan, Penelope Featherington

Kathryn Drysdale, Genevieve Delacroix

Phoebe Dynevor, Daphne Bridgerton

Ruth Gemmell, Violet Bridgerton

Claudia Jessie, Eloise Bridgerton

Jessica Madsen, Cressida Cowper

Luke Newton, Colin Bridgerton

Regé-Jean Page, The Duke of Hastings

Golda Roushevel, Queen Charlotte

Luke Thompson, Benedict Bridgerton

Polly Walker, Portia Featherington

PRODUCTION CREATIVES

Kris Bowers, Composer

Tricia Brock, Director

Jess Brownell, Writer & Producer

Sophie Canale, Season 2 Costume Designer

Holden Chang, Producer, Post Production

Scott Collins, Head of Post Production, Shondaland

Gina Cromwell, Set Decorator

Charlotte Dent, Horse Master

Sam Dent, Horse Master

Cheryl Dunye, Director

Alison Eakle, Chief Content Officer, Shondaland

Greg Evans, Editor, Post Production

Sara Fischer, EVP, Head of Production, Shondaland

Sheree Folkson, Director

Dr. Hannah Greig, Historian

Franki Hackett, Stunts

Will Hughes-Jones, Production Designer

Jane Karen, Dialect Coach

Annie Laks, SVP Creative Content, Shondaland

Sarada McDermott, Season 1 Producer

Ellen Mirojnick, Season 1 Costume Designer

Jack Murphy, Choreographer

Erika Ökvist, Season 2 Hair & Makeup Designer

Alexandra Patsavas, Music Supervisor

Alex Pillai, Director

Julia Quinn, Novelist

Julie Anne Robinson, Director & Executive Producer

Lizzie Talbot, Intimacy Coordinator

Kelly Valentine Hendry, Casting Director

Tom Verica, Senior Creative Production Advisor, Shondaland

Michelle Wright, Season 2 Producer

INTRODUCTION

There is no world like the Bridgerton *world.*

Distinctive and sizzling, the Regency-era show based on the fictional books by Julia Quinn was an unheard-of unicorn—a glamorous period piece that did not take itself too seriously—when it aired on Netflix in December 2020. *Bridgerton* was an instant phenomenon. My producing partner, Betsy Beers, and I have produced hit shows before (*Grey's Anatomy, Scandal, How to Get Away with Murder*), but we had never made anything that grabbed the attention of enormous audiences in countries around the world at the same time. The force of *Bridgerton* is breathtaking to us, and its influence with fans shows no signs of stopping. As we speak, we are hard at work shooting Seasons 3 and 4.

    Bridgerton the series was created by the talented writer Chris Van Dusen. What makes Chris so wonderful is that he brings a unique voice and perspective to the page, filling scenes with humor and wit, warmth and emotion. His gift was *Bridgerton*'s gain.

    I always say that being a show creator is not a simple task. Building a world out of thin air (or, in this case, from the pages of Julia Quinn's books) is an intense challenge. But I also say that no one person ever really creates a show. That has always been true for the shows I created, and that is true for *Bridgerton*. A TV show starts with the brilliance of a script. But a script is a blueprint. The show itself is created by the amazing team of people who work day by day, week by week, during development, production, and post-production to make a television series. There are executives and line producers, actors and directors, set decorators and costume designers, hair and makeup teams, lighting designers and editors, writing staff and (on this show) historians. And more. All those people helped to create the world of *Bridgerton* that you see on your screen.

    Which brings me to this book in your hands. Betsy and I are producers. We played key roles in bringing *Bridgerton* to life, from idea to finished product. We saw firsthand all the extraordinary work done by so many people who helped create this world. And we wanted to celebrate it. We wrote this book to share with you the craftsmanship, effort, and beauty of what went into building the world of *Bridgerton*. We also wrote this book to sneak you a few behind-the-scenes secrets. After all, we could not enter the world of Lady Whistledown without a few whispers of hot gossip, could we? Settle in. Loosen your corset. Gentle Reader, this is for you.

—Shonda Rhimes

NEW YORK, MAY 2022

Once Upon a Time
(in a Hotel Room in Mayfair)

SHONDA: Shall we take everyone back to the beginning? Not to the 1800s but to 2017 and that hotel room where I was sick and needed something to read, and there happened to be a copy of *The Duke & I* by Julia Quinn, the first of the *Bridgerton* novels. I wasn't into romance novels; I really didn't even know much about the genre. But I picked it up, couldn't put it down, and then immediately got my hands on the rest of them because they were fabulous. And then I passed them on to you.

BETSY: I thought you might have hit your head in that hotel room while you had the flu. Romance novels? But you insisted that they would be a fabulous show, and you have excellent taste. I was deeply skeptical because I hadn't read a romance novel since I was a teen—I'd certainly never read a period romance novel.

SHONDA: Totally—you read the ones of the 1980s, when everyone wore huge shoulder pads and diamonds.

BETSY: Right.

SHONDA: Fair—as far as a period romance, if it wasn't Jane Austen, I didn't really know about it. I'm not going to dis Jane Austen because I'm not an idiot . . .

BETSY: She might get upset.

SHONDA: She might roll over in her grave. But Julia Quinn's novels were just so much juicier than Austen's, and they're written by someone who was far less confined and less proper. After all, Julia is a modern woman, not stuck in the constraints of the age.

BETSY: Without a doubt. And I never knew that the ton existed. Austen wrote about a pastoral society where everyone is in relatively drab clothes and spent a lot of time in chapels and churches.

SHONDA: Totally. And they recycled their dresses more.

BETSY: Meanwhile, this was an amazing world of luxury and excess. And she had this crazy device of a gossip columnist pulling the strings, which was such a cool concept. Julia created an entirely new, glamorous, bright world that you had actually never seen before.

SHONDA: It really worked. As did the fact that she built an incredible community that you get to follow over a decade, but each of the eight books is a complete story, focusing on different Bridgerton children as they find love. And she allows people happy endings.

BETSY: We've rarely had that opportunity. We don't have to kill anyone off!

SHONDA: Exactly. We don't have to come up with an unbelievable amount of twists and turns, nobody needs to die. It's funny, because people were so upset when they realized Regé-Jean Page wouldn't be back—but that was the point! He overcame his obstacle, found love, and got his happy ending. And there are so many great stories yet to be told. Julia gave us a map, but there were a couple of ways we could approach source material: We could stick to every book directly, or we could use them simply as jumping-off points. I think we chose somewhere in between.

BETSY: I agree. And she's been an amazing collaborator and so enthusiastic and supportive. It's been great to have her as a constant resource, along with all the historians and experts who have been able to school us in the manners of the time. They created enough structure in some ways for us to be free.

SHONDA: And we took some essential liberties. We immediately started talking about the rumors around Queen Charlotte, that she was actually of African descent, which opened a door in my mind through which the show came to be: not fantasy, just an alternate reality, an alternate version of history. That became a very interesting way to tell this story without belaboring it, or making race "the thing," when really, pleasure, sex, and love are the things.

BETSY: Let's be honest: The "thing" was the idea that Violet Bridgerton had *a thousand* children—by choice—and wants them to all marry for love, when nobody did such a thing. Love was a radical concept at the time rather than *the most important thing.*

SHONDA: It's funny to think about this now, because we are a romantic society—love is the most important thing, and then you figure out the rest. It feels almost incomprehensible to marry someone today who you didn't love, whereas it was a rarity in Regency England. Certainly worthy of the gossip columns. The driving factors in the marriage mart were wealth and status—and many hoped to find a man who would give them an heir and then, ideally, die. It's wild to imagine that the ultimate promise of marriage was eventual widowhood.

BETSY: I kind of get it, though, because Lady Danbury is goals. But these Bridgertons and their love of love keep breaking that mold. They are the bridge from period to modern storytelling in the show; we relate to them. And this is important, because we were looking for all the connective tissue we could find to create a world that audiences today could project themselves into, characters who they could say, "That's me." People could really relate and find someone in that family to relate to, whether it was Eloise, Daphne, Benedict, or Anthony. And then, of course, there are their counterparts: There are a lot of people who feel like they are Kate.

SHONDA: Exactly. Shall we take people back to the beginning, beginning now?

Julia Quinn on Getting THE CALL from Her Agent

I think we all have moments in our lives we would love to relive over and over again, and one of mine is when I got the call from my agent that Shondaland wanted to adapt the *Bridgerton* novels. It was a fairy-tale story of everything going right. There were signs at every stage that Shondaland was paying attention and working things through on their end, and that maybe I would actually see the world of *Bridgerton* come alive on the screen.

I could tell, based on the questions that were coming, that everyone at Shondaland had read the books very carefully and understood the implications of how interconnected the world could be. They were crystal clear about which books and which *characters* they wanted. Everything about

it was fabulous, beyond my wildest dreams.

And I want to make a fine point on that, because my dreams are not small—but I never, ever thought that I would see something like this happen to one of my books. Nobody makes historical romances into television series or movies. If someone wants to make a period piece, they make *Pride and Prejudice* . . . again. There's prestige attached to Jane Austen. If you can put a spin on her brilliance, then that makes you a visionary. Nobody was looking to contemporarily written historical romance novels as source material.

Let's be honest: It's a genre that's written primarily by women. It's read primarily by women. It's edited primarily by women. And you have a film industry where, up

until recently, it's been primarily men making decisions. Women's work and joy have never been valued in the same way as men's work and joy. Interestingly, those are themes in the books as well.

I gave up creative control—not because I don't trust myself or care about the result but because I am not going to be the person to tell Shonda Rhimes how to make television. I had every faith—and for good reason—that she would know exactly how to translate the books into television. And as I also came to know Betsy Beers and Chris Van Dusen, I had even more faith that Shonda's vision of my vision would be realized.

Before Betsy sent me the first script, she called to warn me that it would be structured a bit differently and open a bit differently than the books—that in some ways, they needed to teach the audience about romance novels. I thought that was interesting but steeled myself nonetheless, expecting that I would be a little disappointed. But when it landed in my in-box, I took my computer to the corner of my house where I could be alone and read it, grinning the entire time.

It was utterly brilliant. Different, yes, but beautifully done in a way that I never would have considered. It was perfect.

Shonda & Betsy on Giving the Romance Genre the Props It Deserves

SHONDA: There is a serious lack of respect for the romance genre in Hollywood—if we have any part in blowing that up and showing the incredible potential of this material, I will be very happy. Because the fans are incredible, and they deserve to see what they love on television. It was my greatest hope that we could give the fans of these books something they thought was worthy—while also expanding it into three dimensions.

BETSY: Yes, we had an incredible opportunity to not only serve Julia Quinn's fan base but also draw in an entirely new crowd, a group of people who maybe had preconceived ideas about the romance genre. And what we witnessed was the reverse of what typically happens with book-to-TV or -movie translations: People rushed out to buy the books after watching the show. Usually, it's the opposite!

SHONDA: I mean, how amazing is it that we gave people a hunger—or I should say thirst—to read books. That's the best thing ever.

BETSY: I think the best thing ever is that, hopefully, romance novels will no longer be relegated to "silly lady" fiction.

SHONDA: Isn't it interesting how, invariably, if women are really into something, that thing is automatically downgraded in category and shoved into a corner. But when men like something that women don't understand, it's still vaunted, valued, and special. Look at comic books: People who don't like comic books have an "ugh" reaction, but because they're typically loved by men, they have a very lauded place in our storytelling genre. We can't stop making comic book adaptations—while romance books have been excluded from the screen.

BETSY: What's interesting to me is that a lot of women like Marvel movies in the same way that a lot of gentlemen were fully engaged with *Bridgerton*—and did not need to be dragged to the table. It's amazing how many men had a lot to say about the show: They were invested.

SHONDA: As they should be!

BRIDGERTON PRODUCTION HISTORIAN
DR. HANNAH GREIG ON THE REGENCY WORLD

Our primary reference points for Regency England are Jane Austen novels, where we don't typically get references to dukes or duchesses or members of the royal family. Mr. Darcy and Mrs. Bennet, whom we know so well from Austen's *Pride and Prejudice,* have no titles—they were not in the world of lords and ladies. We would describe the people who populate Austen's novels as upper middle class: The fathers and brothers might be in business, or they might be clergymen or in the military; and they don't necessarily own huge country houses, which were typically owned by earls, counts, lords, and dukes. The homes that we see in Austen are medium-sized, if you can believe it. It's a slightly different perspective on what it was like to be wealthy in the eighteenth century, a very different world than the English aristocracy in *Bridgerton.*

The English aristocracy, or "peerage," is actually a very small group—a few hundred families—though immensely powerful, structured around inherited titles. Duke/duchess is the highest rank that you can have, followed by marquess/marchioness, earl/countess, viscount/viscountess, then baron/baroness. Lady and lord apply to anyone in the peerage, though if someone is a duke, you are supposed to refer to him by his title. These titles are either bestowed by the monarchy or passed from father to son. It's a patriarchal society and therefore run by men.

Not only did these men hold all the wealth, they also dominated government. In the Bridgerton family, Anthony holds the title of viscount, but Benedict, Colin, and Gregory would be untitled and expected to make their own way in the world.

They would need careers, potentially in the military or in the clergy. They might find themselves in business in some way, or they could represent the family in parliament. This is where Daphne's marriage is quite useful to the family, as the Duke of Hastings has a lot of money and therefore a lot of control over things like seats in parliament. The duke could be very useful to the brothers by setting them up in careers and securing their futures. This is also how the circle of society effectively kept itself small and contained, by ensuring that outsiders never penetrated its power structures.

That small circle also meant the wealth stayed among these families. The members of the ton were rich. Filthy rich. For perspective, Jane Austen's wealthy but untitled hero Mr. Darcy was famously said to be worth £10,000 per year as an annual income, which would be loosely equivalent to £5 million per year (not too shabby!). Well, the wealthiest member of Regency high society, including the mega-rich dukes, cleared ten times that in the early 1800s, around £100,000 per year of annual income. Yep, that's £50 million (!!!!) in today's money. They were almost incalculably wealthy compared to everyone else. They drew income from their vast estates in England, but they also held land abroad, including plantations worked by enslaved people. For context of their immense privilege, a domestic maid might earn £3 per year (plus free board and lodging)—a paltry £1,500 by today's standards—while a working family in the textile industry or similar might command £15 per year across the family members (£7,500 today).

WRITING THE WORLD

SHONDA: So I found Chris Van Dusen first. He was my assistant on the first season of *Grey's Anatomy.* As he tells the story, we were supposed to meet on a bench on the lot, and he was late, which is very unlike Chris.

BETSY: Thank God you forgave him, because he really has been with us since the beginning. Chris is just one of those people who can really do anything: He's incredibly creative and always applies so much effort to any task.

SHONDA: *Bridgerton* was one of my passion projects, but I knew I couldn't take on writing these seasons by myself without putting us seriously behind schedule—Violet has so many children! Chris Van Dusen is one of us, and I knew I could trust him to build this world and execute on our collective vision.

BETSY: It really was a wonderful collaboration: You just can't put on a show of this scale—on another continent, in another time period—without a lot of teamwork. And Chris's initial outline was brilliant. One of the defining features of any Shondaland script is the stage directions, and in the first few pages, you know exactly what the show is about. All the nondialogue writing gives you the tone of the show.

CHRIS VAN DUSEN: Shonda told me about the *Bridgerton* books, which I had never heard of before. I took them home that first night and read the first one in a matter of hours. I read the second book the next night, and so on. I was hooked.

I'm a huge fan of the genre in part because there are all these rules that men and women of the time had to follow. They all knew exactly what was expected of them and how to behave and not to behave. It's perfect for storytelling because it's confined. I wanted to stay true to the time of Regency but also modernize the world and explore these characters and stories through a contemporary lens. It works because the stories themselves are timeless and universal. We know these people because they are us. In period clothing.

It's a spirited show with daring people who talk really fast. The banter is sharp and witty and at times really, really sexy. We do like to leave viewers a little hot and bothered! You don't always get that in your more traditional period pieces.

We wanted a freshness and youthfulness to everything, with lots of sparkle and effervescence. The volume is literally turned up. But at the same time, the show thrives in the space of being relatable to whoever's watching, no matter who you are. It's also Shondaland, so having such a diverse group of characters affords us the ability to explore such an array of storylines. Race is as much a part of the show's conversation as class and gender are.

SHONDALAND CHIEF CONTENT OFFICER ALISON EAKLE: I immediately understood why Shonda was so excited—as a development executive and a former writer, I could see that the series maps perfectly to an eight-season show. Every story deserves its own unfurling. Each is contained in a single book, and yet the books contain an extensive world and community that you can come back to again and again. It's truly brilliant and made for TV.

We finalized the rights deal with Netflix, got their blessing, and finally, Betsy, Shonda, and I sat down with Chris Van Dusen, handed him *The Duke & I*, and asked him to dig in.

STAFFING THE ROOM:

Putting a writers' room together is an act of complex chemistry: Budget is one limiting factor, but because it's Shondaland, and we write the world as we know it, we also wanted to ensure we had lots of different points of view in the room. The *Bridgerton* room included seasoned vets and first-time writers. Some staffers are excellent on the page, others are really strong in the writers' room, and then you always want someone who is terrific on set.

We preread hundreds of writers to be sure that we could cover all our key needs: Are they funny? Can they write something with a lot of heat? Honestly, most writers can't do both—it's hard to be simultaneously witty and raunchy. It really came down to finding people who could do a bit of both, or overindexed strongly in one direction.

We had the room going for about six months. You take the first few weeks to really think about the big picture and what the season—and, ultimately, the series—should look like, because you need to plant threads that can later be picked up and woven into fuller stories. You're looking for the spine of the season and the trajectory of various characters. Then you assign out episodes to different writers, though many things are written together in the room as a group. In our writers' rooms, you either succeed together or you all fail.

Character Development

SHONDA: The two prevailing factors in every single one of our shows are that we create characters that people want to watch, and we put those characters in impossible situations and then watch them work their way out of them.

BETSY: One of the things I've always loved about the way you tell stories is that you force people to get to know these characters as multidimensional people who might surprise them. We go on a real roller coaster through the seasons with Anthony: At first he seems like a stubborn rake until we learn about a profound childhood wound that makes him fearful of attachment. I certainly feel that way about Lady Featherington, who really changes our understanding of her over time. You may not like what she does, but you come to understand that she does what she does for very good reasons. Daphne grows facets of personality in Season 1, like when she takes what she wants from Simon in bed. It *seems* out of character, but the reality is that we're all complex, not just dutiful and obliging daughters, not just social-climbing nutjobs, not just selfish bachelors.

SHONDA: Totally. I very much felt that way about Lady Featherington when she takes Marina to the poor neighborhood and effectively says, "Do you want to end up like this?" As her marriage unravels, you recognize that she had to make a similar choice—a loveless marriage to a man who barely acknowledges her. She is doing the best that she can. This is her life. You feel her trauma, whereas at the beginning she's just sort of mean, and laughable, and slightly repulsive, and very, very funny.

BETSY: Those Featheringtons are hilarious *and* full of feeling. Marina also takes us on a bit of a ride: I certainly sympathized with her at the end, whereas I despised her a little bit at points. And even Simon: When we meet him in the beginning, he has a stick up his ass. But then you learn about his childhood, and you start to understand why he's so guarded and fearful of intimacy—watching all of this unfold informs the way you look at these characters, the same way you come to know people in real life over time.

REGENCY SLANG

RAKE: playboy or womanizer

TENANT FOR LIFE: marry for life

DICKED IN THE KNOB: crazy

FOXED: drunk

DIPPING RATHER DEEP: drinking heavily

DRUNK AS A WHEELBARROW: very drunk

A SIDESLIP OR BYBLOW: child out of wedlock

A SLIP OF A GIRL: a lithe woman

CUT DIRECT: a very deliberate public snub
where someone looks away or refuses to
acknowledge and address you

ALL THE CRACK: very fashionable

BLUNT: money

HALF LOVE: immature love of a young woman

HIGH IN THE INSTEP: arrogant

DAMN TUM: false rumor, lie, or trick

PROMENADE: a walk in public for attention,
not exercise

FACER: punching someone in the face

LEG SHACKLE: marriage

DIAMOND OF THE FIRST WATER: the most
desirable debutante, peerless, without flaw

Shonda on the Addition of Queen Charlotte to the World

The addition of Queen Charlotte was useful as we wrote and created this world. She became a way for us to expand the view of people of color in that society. We could populate the show in a way that was different from your usual period piece. And we could portray the grace and grandeur of our queen. We understand the power of the monarchy and we respect it. So we were able to decide right away that this Queen Charlotte existed in a *Bridgerton* universe and did not need to be an exact representation of the actual Queen Charlotte. This freed us to tell the story the way we needed to tell it.

The story behind our *Bridgerton* story is that there were two separate societies moving forward in London—a white society and a Black society—and when Queen Charlotte and King George III fell in love, he decided to unite the societies and granted land and titles. Simple.

What became very interesting to me in Season 1 is the concept that Simon's father was obsessed with this idea of an heir, and that their position in society was tenuous enough that it could be pulled away at any minute if he did not have someone to whom he could pass along his land and title—yet he did not understand the unifying force of love. And if he were to stop obsessing and look around and see his son and the world as it was remade, he would realize that the most powerful people in the room are all of color.

A wonderful side effect of adding Queen Charlotte to this world is that we are getting a window into the lonely life of this character. Queen Charlotte is surrounded by people all of the time yet seems to be uniquely lonely.

We begin to understand that, even for her, a woman's power is derived from the social scene. The marriage mart is the "workplace" of the Regency-era woman. And for Queen Charlotte, it is the perfect playground to keep her life exciting.

CHRIS VAN DUSEN: In the writers' room, we started from the place of making the story relevant to today. I wanted it to be a running modern commentary about how, in the last two hundred years, everything has changed while nothing has changed at all. We had some really spirited debates in that room about the roles of men and women! We always joked that there are no dating apps, obviously, but at these balls, they were still swiping left and right until the early-morning hours. Finding all those modern references was really fun.

WRITER AND PRODUCER JESS BROWNELL:
That was the key as we began to write: We wrote them just as we would a modern character, and then we went back and made it cohere to the period in terms of the mannerisms of speech. On a show like *Grey's Anatomy* or *Scandal*, when we might not have the right medical or political terminology or jargon, we would write the *emotion* of the scene. Then we would go back with the research and make it accurate. The same process held with *Bridgerton*, we just went back through it and made it period-appropriate.

So, for example, if Simon said something like, "Oh, I'm drunk"; then, after we had gone through all the research, we might change that to something like, "Oh, I'm foxed." If you're talking about someone having a child out of wedlock, you would replace it with "sideslip." We ultimately came to realize that we didn't need to be experts in how these people talked: We could just focus on the narrative and the emotion of the scene and then fill in the historical details after.

ALISON EAKLE: This was our first project at Netflix, and it was also the first time that we had the opportunity to write an entire season before casting the show. Typically, we are writing a show as it shoots, building the plane while it is already in flight, and using the actors' performances to play to their strengths or to follow their intuition. The magic of writing them all at once is that you have the chance to edit as you discover things about the characters, as they shift and evolve. You get to go back and tweak scripts and set things up. The only script that wasn't finalized by the time we started shooting was Episode Eight, because we needed the time to determine exactly how to tie up the season while teeing up the next. And let's be clear: At Shondaland, happy endings are new to us! It took us a minute to find our feet.

JESS BROWNELL: When we think about Regency-era characters having sex, it feels really foreign; we think of people from olden times as being quite prim and proper, in those Empire-waist dresses and waistcoats, but of course, our understanding of earlier times is a historian's perspective of that era—and, well, they likely had the same prudish manners. While writing *Bridgerton,* we pretty much determined that Regency people had the same urges and were just as lusty as everyone today. Add repression to this mix, and you can imagine that most people were about to combust with unexpressed sexual desire.

Speaking of prolonged desire, in most romance novels, everything is quite tepid until three quarters of the way through, when the protagonists get married and suddenly there are "maidenheads" and "warriors" everywhere. We didn't think we could string people along for six episodes, and so the dream sequence, for example, came about because we wanted to bring some thirst in a bit earlier—we didn't want them to wait until Episode Six to touch and hold each other. It also offered a good way to get into Daphne's head, so the audience could get a sense of her simmering desire.

We talked a lot about Daphne's arc—not just in her character but also in her arc within the sex scenes, which are very narrative. They are not gratuitous at all, they are essential. They really drive her evolution and development from a prudish girl who doesn't know anything to a woman who owns her desire, who comes to know herself intimately and starts to ask for what she wants. She wants a child, yes, but she also wants to have sex in less traditional positions or, you know, out on the grass in the rain. She begins to realize that her life is her own, and sex became a great way for us to tell that story.

Once we got past our own giggling and blushing, it was quite fun to write all those sex scenes. I remember sitting in my office one night writing one, and I was really getting into it. My head was down, I was in a flow state, and I had a sudden revelation that I was effectively writing porn. Pages and pages of "breath-hovering" porn. And that my boss was going to read this, and if he was expecting me to write, "And then they have sex," this was going to be quite embarrassing for me.

I went into Chris's office and asked, "How much detail are you expecting from the sex scenes?" And his classic response was, "Oh, I want detail." It was definitely one of the most awkward moments of my career, similar to how Daphne must have felt when she asked her mom how babies are made. Chris challenged me to choreograph every movement, to write down every single action item: The action lines are *very* descriptive and colorful.

JESS BROWNELL: Throughout the show, we wrote from the female point-of-view—I think many feminist sex stories sometimes wander down a woman's body because they forget that they're supposed to stick with the woman's gaze. That was very important to us, to be consistent to Daphne and her perspective. I don't think anything we did was gratuitous, but we wanted to make these moments simply because they were departures from what you typically see: In *Bridgerton,* when Simon drops trou, Daphne moves her gaze down his body. Her eyes light up, and as a viewer, you remember that she has been completely shielded from any understanding of sex: She's, like, seen paintings of naked men in galleries, but certainly not in real life! And not in the same room! Her reaction to Simon's naked body is very pure.

As we were writing, we kept shaking ourselves out of the historical context, which would have us believe that everyone was kind of asexual—prim and proper and absent of all desires. But we wanted to remind viewers that they are horny, too. Their eyes light up when they see a naked man. This was a realization that allowed us to access these characters and write them as if we were writing a modern character. They are human!

ALISON EAKLE ON THE ISSUE OF CONSENT:

We had a big conversation with Netflix about Episode Six, when Daphne decides to get on top of Simon and clamp down. They obviously flagged the issue of consent and told us that if we left it as it was, the entire season would be marked as containing sexual violence. It does say "Sexual Violence" on every single episode.

But that was a crucial, crucial moment, one that we had already adapted from the book to make it more understandable from Daphne's perspective. She is in a moment where she is trying to understand the truth—she has been lied to and is figuring it out. Ultimately, we decided that we would accept the warning label because we needed to have that moment. And there absolutely are consent issues around Daphne and Simon's moment. It's 1813, so they are not going to talk about consent in real time, but the injury is palpable.

In the book, Daphne gets Simon drunk, versus our version, where in the moment she just decides to go for it: She wanted to understand if that was the thing he was not being real with her about. The idea of her getting him drunk felt more problematic— we wanted it to be a sober event.

The Season:
OTHERWISE KNOWN AS THE MARRIAGE MART

DR. HANNAH GREIG: In the world of *Bridgerton*, people know who they are and what is expected of them, particularly the ton.

It's hard to understand the amount of pressure that this high-society world places on both men and women . . . *especially* women. They've been brought up to understand: You have one season, about six months of balls, to play the game well and win the person you're theoretically going to spend your life with. And you must do this under the watchful eyes of your "ambitious mama" and the rest of society. If you failed to secure a match, then you were old hat by the following season. This is why Daphne is so intent on getting it right—she's the first in her family to wed, and a great match will ensure that her younger sisters can make great matches, too.

As Lady Bridgerton and Daphne head to Lady Danbury's ball, the first of the season, you can feel the pressure: Like for all her peers, the clock is ticking. You enter the marriage mart in your late teens, but when you hit twenty-seven, the door fully shuts, and you are a designated spinster. The season is exciting, certainly, but Daphne needs to secure her value in the marriage mart by finding a great match—she knows that this is her path to full agency and power.

While the marriage mart seems restrictive, it's also important to remember that securing a good match ensured a semblance of freedom for women. Many women lived separately from their husbands, had male friends, and could go freely from place to place. And, of course, the best game of marriage is the one where your rich husband dies, leaving you with a young heir to the estate, meaning you have decades of doing exactly as you please—Lady Trowbridge, with her toddler son, is the perfect example.

SHONDA AND BETSY ON THE WACKINESS OF THE MARRIAGE MART:

SHONDA: It's easy to think of something like the marriage mart as a relic of another time and place, but it's worth remembering that we still have a culture of debutantes in America—and there's an actual Social Register, a list of fancy, pedigreed individuals, that still exists. There are certainly families who continue to be fixated on making advantageous matches. And while there might not be dowries, the idea of marriage as a way to accrue social power and status remains.

BETSY: It feels so outrageous. You could argue, though, that it's equivalent to sizing up prospective spouses based on their abilities as a co-parent and their earning potential—but even then we like to consider those as afterthoughts, as nice-to-haves and not essential. Love comes first. In some ways, it's the reverse of what we see in the ton, where

finding a spouse who can secure your safety and security is strictly about strategy. Happiness is not a consideration.

SHONDA: This is what makes the Bridgerton family and the *Bridgerton* books so compelling—within this wider society that's constrained by obligation and social mores, they primarily care about love. Daphne isn't focused on rank, she wants friendship *and*, though she can't express it, *desire.* Daphne and Simon burn for each other in a world that's typically ice cold. Love matches are so rare, it would seem, that theirs is the "one" of the season. Anthony, meanwhile, just wants to dispatch with his duty and find his match—to perform according to expectations of the time. His mom pulls him toward love.

BETSY: Perhaps because nobody else lives within families that prioritize love, Anthony and Daphne's peers wouldn't even know what to look for—and so following the rules of society might feel quite sensible to them, like to-dos you cross off the list. In a way, I kind of understand the comfort in that, too. Writer and producer Jess Brownell thinks that the marriage mart has its upsides: If someone dances with you twice, you *know* they're interested. And there can't be much ghosting when your relationship is under a microscope—if a man makes his interest known, it seems like he will be coerced to follow through.

Anatomy of a Scene
SEASON 1: PRESENTATION DAY

DIRECTOR: JULIE ANNE ROBINSON   •   EPISODE: 101—"DIAMOND OF THE FIRST WATER"

"We only had enough people in that room to fill half, so we used the same people twice—we pushed them onto the other side of the room and shot them again."

—Will Hughes-Jones

CHRIS VAN DUSEN: The presentation scene was a wild day. We essentially had the entire cast present, everyone in white with feathers everywhere, at the most beautiful location: Wilton House in Salisbury. One of my favorite shots in the show is a tracking shot where we move toward the queen and her ladies-in-waiting from Daphne's point of view: She's walking down the aisle toward what is effectively a firing squad.

Golda is up there being imperious. Just judging. I had a specific image in my head of how I wanted the queen and her ladies to be arranged on the podium, which made that shot important for several reasons, in part because it's our introduction to the most powerful person in the show.

I pulled Julie Anne Robinson aside before we filmed and showed her a GIF from Beyoncé's "Formation" video. I told her it was in my head while I was writing that scene, because it has such a sense of power, an almost intimidating undercurrent of energy. It's one of my favorite shots from the show.

Notes and Rewrites

SHONDA: Usually, my job is to fully create a show from the blank page. But with *Bridgerton*, I was able to act as sort of a "super-showrunner" to a new creator, Chris Van Dusen. I loved that role. Chris and I talked endlessly about the show before he even wrote a word. Then, as he wrote, he would email me questions or drop by my office to ask for my opinion on story plans for the writers' room. Once the scripts were written, my job was to read every script and give notes. I would do that on my laptop at all hours. I write my notes directly in the scripts—in little yellow note bubbles. Sometimes the notes were small, like dialogue changes for Lady Whistledown or changes to how Violet says a line that might make for more clarity. And sometimes the notes were bigger, like the direction of an entire episode or a scene.

For the first episode of *Bridgerton*, I remember feeling strongly about the scene with Daphne and Anthony riding in the park. I felt Daphne needed to express the complexities that came from her role in society. I knew we needed that beat to understand her and, frankly, to respect her from the perspective of twenty-first-century viewers. Because someone so dedicated to "finding a man" was *not* quite the ideal Shondaland character. In Shondaland, our women are empowered and independent. So we needed to show that Daphne is empowered and independent, too—but in a *Regency way*. Her power and her independence are based on the freedom and status one receives with marriage. Which may sound strange to our modern ears. But that is how it was. The marriage mart was the focus for women. It was, in essence, their "workplace"—the same way a hospital or a fixer's firm or a law firm has been a traditional workplace for our characters. It is where they found their successes and failures—where women deal in power. And I wanted all of that conveyed in one short monologue that Daphne gives while riding through the park with her brother.

So I wrote: "And what of my duty? You have no idea what it is to be a woman. What it might feel like to have one's life reduced to a single moment. This is all I have been raised for. This is all I am. I have no other value. If I am unable to find a husband, I shall be useless."

A larger idea that I shared as part of my notes on the first episode—I had Chris do a pass on the script that made it clear how naive the women in the show are about sex. We needed to show it as a taboo subject that left our young ladies thoroughly uneducated on the topic. I wanted to make sure our audience was clear about the rules of our world, and how the women are left in the dark was key to the way this world works. This concept is especially important to the main story of the season. If the audience did not understand that Daphne was sexually uneducated, the story points on which her romance with the duke hinged would not land. So Chris worked hard to find ways to convey the innocence of young women in terms of reproduction.

> *Just for dialogue purposes: "Should your brother want to be obeyed as Lord Bridgerton, he should need to ACT as Lord Bridgerton." Or some such thing to make clear what she means. Or do we want to make this a bigger deal? Violet is downright NERVOUS because of the sensation it will cause for Daphne to be presented without her guardian present?*

EXT. GRASSY WOODLAND - DAY

> *Is there a valet standing by? Catching Anthony's eye about the time? Which is what makes him check his pocket watch? I think it would be delightful if there were a valet and a maid out there forced to wait in the woodlands hearing all of this.*

Where we find a ravenous ANTHONY BRIDGERTON (28), along with a lady friend -- SIENA ROSSO (20s) -- up against a tree. His breeches, down around his boots. Her skirts, bunched around her waist. When Anthony reaches out to check his POCKET-WATCH. Unhappy, he tosses the watch aside. And as his movements seem to grow *a tad bit faster*, we move...

EXT. MAYFAIR - DAY

As horses RUMBLE through these early 19th century streets...

              LADY WHISTLEDOWN (V.O.)
      For today is the day London's marriage-   ★
      minded misses shall be presented to   ★
      Her Majesty the Queen...   ★

CARRIAGES wind their ways past grand, scenic architecture: CARLTON HOUSE. PICCADILLY. An UNDER-CONSTRUCTION BUCKINGHAM HOUSE (not yet Palace)...   ★

INT. BRIDGERTON CARRIAGE/EXT. MAYFAIR - DAY

As a beaming Daphne eyes the beautiful scenery that passes...   ★

              LADY WHISTLEDOWN (V.O.)
      A much anticipated day, when dreams   ★
      shall finally be achieved. Hopes,   ★
      fully realized.   ★

A proud Violet smiles, next to a giddy Hyacinth, a reserved   ★
Francesca and a Whistledown-reading Eloise.

INT. FEATHERINGTON CARRIAGE/EXT. MAYFAIR - DAY

As Prudence and Philipa vie for space in their seats and an indifferent Penelope plays with her HAIR RIBBON.

              LADY WHISTLEDOWN (V.O.)
      And courses of lives, changed. For   ★
      the better. *One should hope.*   ★

ALISON EAKLE: Shonda and Chris would dig in and talk through where she had different ideas or spots in the script that needed to be rearranged. This is Shonda's genius: She is incredible at structure. She is also finicky about the rules of Regency England and very intimate with the romance genre, so she flagged scenes like the boxing match in Season 1, which initially featured Daphne attending with the prince to watch half-naked men fight, which would, in reality at the time, ruin a lady. But because she was chaperoned on her date with the prince by her brothers, the historians said it was kosher.

Shonda doesn't rewrite, she fills up scripts with little thought bubbles that might read, "This piece of dialogue feels false and this is why . . ." or "This scene should move over there because . . ." And she's always right. While I can often flag something that isn't going to work for Shonda, I can never anticipate the solution.

Netflix also gave great notes—some that we narratively or functionally couldn't address, but they called out some key things.

One note they offered significantly altered the show for the better. In the original script, we had Simon in the "Dark Walk," adjacent to Vauxhall Gardens, with Siena. He had left the ball to find some action! Anthony, in an effort to force himself to get rid of Siena, had set the two of them up. Ultimately, when Simon emerges, stumbling out of the darkness, he is putting his jacket back on when he comes across Daphne "planting a facer" on Nigel. Well, Netflix did not love that: They felt like it was a really hard character beat for Simon to recover from. Here you have Siena, handed over like a piece of property by Anthony—which, let's be honest, she effectively was in such a scenario—and then you have the juxtaposition of Simon being *very* rakish with Siena to having that beautifully romantic dance with Daphne. They felt it was too much. And they were absolutely right, because it would have taken people out of the story right at a key moment when you're building to something incredible. Their pitch was that he had simply left the ball to escape the ambitious mamas, and in the edit, it works.

"*Shonda was convinced that, as a longtime Shondaland writer, Chris could carry her vision for the show across the finish line. And he nailed it in the outline—I was on my way to bed on a school night when it landed in my in-box, and I had to head straight for the couch instead. Suddenly, I was in a Regency-era music video, flying through Mayfair—even in the outline, you could feel the tone and vibe of the show. It was the perfect prototype for the season: spicy, modern, and yet it managed to feel Regency, too, but completely unlike any other version of that period.*"

—Alison Eakle

Anatomy of a Scene
THE BIRTHING SCENE

DIRECTOR: ALEX PILLAI • EPISODE: 203—"A BEE IN YOUR BONNET"

BETSY BEERS: One of the most interesting journeys in Season 2 is Violet's, and the way she comes to acknowledge her culpability in the situation with Anthony because of how she fell apart and disappeared after her husband's death. That was definitely a situation—in terms of editing—of tonnage. We had a lot of footage that Chris was working through that was just *torture*. We had to ask ourselves, "How much do we want this to resonate? And how much do we want to feel for Violet and, at the same point, not lose traction in the story?" Originally, we had more moments like the one in the drawing room where she says to Anthony, "You'll understand why I can't have lunch with the family."

Shonda looked at that chunk of the episode, and the scene that was most important to her, which I love, too, was the birthing scene. It told you everything that you need to know: Here is a grieving woman giving birth and dying, and she has no agency or ability to determine the fate of her life or her baby's life. And her young, inexperienced, shell-shocked kid is brought into the room by the doctor to make that decision. To me, that justifies everything that Violet does. After that, you understand.

One of Shonda's points of storytelling brilliance—and Chris has this, too—is that you always understand every character's point of view. The audience understands why people do what they do, or that they at least do what they do for reasons that they feel are incredibly important. Because we all walk around with preconceived notions about who people are, and so much of what we do at Shondaland is flip that on its side. So you think Anthony is one thing in Season 1, and then

you see him in Season 2 and your entire perception of him changes. You get hyper-pissed at Violet, and then you find out what Violet went through. We always populate our world with *people*—not heroes and villains.

RUTH GEMMELL: I don't have children, and so I've never given birth. I needed to be able to feel that I got something physically right before I could add on layers of grief. And so they hired an amazing midwife named Penny to come in and talk to me and work with me. They put us in a hotel, and it was during COVID, and so the hotel was absolutely empty. We went into the dining room, where I virtually went through all the stages of labor. If anyone had come in and wandered around, they would have heard me screaming. Penny really helped me feel safe in the physicality of labor so that I could focus on my grief—because my grief was the anchor for that scene.

ALEX PILLAI: So I actually shot this scene on my birthday, which felt very appropriate, because that scene is really about the universality of the childbirth experience for many women—and many women today, where the mortality rate for mothers is still very high.

It was such an intense experience. Fortunately, Ruth is a very generous actor, and she just went with it—this ferocious mama bear who is also terrified. Because she's in the midst of a life-or-death situation on both accounts, and the doctor keeps looking to her teenage son to make a decision. And ultimately, he doesn't make a decision—he slides out of it.

It was also very technically challenging, because it needed to be raining outside, and we were shooting in a very, very old building called West Wickham, and they would not allow us to make it rain on the outside of the building. So we needed to achieve the effect by projecting what looked like a rain storm onto the windows in order to create that feeling of being an elemental birthing moment.

JONATHAN BAILEY: Those flashback scenes were a very anxious place to be. Because of the intensity of the emotion, Ruth and I had to balance it out with a lot of laughter and crying when we weren't doing the action. There's also something quite amazing about seeing us dressed to look ten years younger. It was thrilling to do those scenes, really, and to be Anthony in those moments when he's buckling under the pressure of his responsibilities and has no idea what he's feeling outside of grief and fear.

SHONDA: The birthing scene in episode 203 was another key scene that I had strong feelings about. We shot much more than you see on-screen, but I wanted to give enough in the script to allow us to have something to play with in the editing room. I felt we needed to convey a different kind of grieving woman in Violet. I didn't want her whimpering or frail. To me, she is strong and fierce. I wanted her grief to be strong and fierce. And it was also clear to me that this woman is a warrior when it came to birth—after all, Violet has eight children. She's not new to childbirth, and she would definitely not be afraid. So I wanted us to have a scene that allowed her to be raging and powerful while she is in the worst labor of her life. We see her anger at death and her command over her own situation. And we get to see how furious she is that these key decisions about women are left to men.

NOTE (put here for me): I feel strongly that
the Violet giving birth scene needs to be rewritten so it
doesn't seem like Violet is confused about where her husband
is or seems whiny. But mostly so it captures a real woman.
 She's a fierce mama bear giving birth for the EIGHTH time.
It's not like she doesn't know how to do this. She's done
it A LOT. And maybe there's something wrong. Maybe it's a
breech birth. But even that she can handle, yelling at the
doctor to reach in and grab both feet. It's not that.
 She's ANGRY. She's HURT and FURIOUS that the man who was
to be by her side until they were old and grey has deserted
her and left her to do this alone. Oh, this is a Violet
worthy of the character. This is the strong rage of a woman
whose dream is dead. Not weak whines.

Violet's on the bed, knees apart under a sheet, howling,
with ANOTHER DOCTOR crouched below. MAIDS stand by, looking
terrified. Anthony hangs back.

> MIDWIFE
> Ma'am, you must wait--

> VIOLET
> --I must PUSH!

Doctor 1 turns to Anthony, quiet and grave:

> DOCTOR 1
> The baby is not in the right position.

> ANTHONY
> What does that mean?

> VIOLET
> What are you saying? What is he
> saying, Anthony--

> DOCTOR 2
> --Just continue to breathe, my lady.

Anthony stands there, wide-eyed.

> VIOLET
> (to the Doctors)
> TELL ME what is the problem?

> DOCTOR 2
> It is... facing the wrong way, ma'am.

> VIOLET
> My baby?

> ANTHONY
> You must do something.

DOCTOR 2
There is nothing--

VIOLET
--REACH IN AND PULL IT OUT!

DOCTOR 1
(to the midwife)
She needs more laudanum.

VIOLET
WHAT I NEED IS FOR YOU TO GET THIS
CHILD OUT OF ME!

MIDWIFE
Breathe, breathe, ma'am.

As Doctor 2 gets to work under the sheet--

DOCTOR 2
(to Violet)
Easy now, easy--

Violet lets out a GUTTURAL SCREAM. Because Doctor 2 is now
attempting to reposition the baby. Anthony has to turn away,
he's so terrified at what's happening.

DOCTOR 2 (CONT'D)
There. THERE!
(then)
It is time to push--

VIOLET
I... I... *Anthony*--

And now she's holding out her hand. For *him*. Anthony pauses,
then rushes to her side. Grabbing her hand. Violet lets
out another WAIL--

DOCTOR 2
Push now. Yes, push! Another!

Another wail, another push, Violet gripping Anthony's hand
as he looks like he wants to be sick. Finally, A BABY'S CRY
fills the room. As Violet strains to stay lucid, the Doctors
and Midwife do their thing--

MIDWIFE
It is... a girl. A healthy girl.

And now Violet's ferociousness subsides. And she begins to
SOB. As BABY HYACINTH is placed into Anthony's arms. He
stares at her, dazed, looking back to Violet.

Creating Lady Whistledown

"Everyone enjoys secrets. Otherwise, why would
Lady Whistledown's paper be so successful?"

—Lady Danbury

JULIA QUINN: I distinctly remember creating Lady Whistledown—I was trying to avoid what writers call an "info dump," which is that need in the first chapter to fill the reader in on everything that they need to know about the time, the place, and the players.

For example, the reader needed to know that Daphne has seven brothers and sisters, and that they're all named alphabetically; they needed to know that her father is dead; they needed to get a sense of her mother. It's very clunky and hard to do that through dialogue and conversation, because these are things that no one would ever recount in real life, in real time.

I had the sudden inspiration that I could kick off the book with an excerpt from a gossip column—an info dump makes sense in that context, as that's exactly what it's meant to be. So I wrote the first column, and then it made sense that Daphne and Violet would discuss it, and Lady Whistledown took off from there as more than just a device for the intro.

I had written about eight chapters and left them on my computer. My dad was visiting, and he just sat down and read the whole thing without my permission. I scolded him, and he responded with the only phrase that you can use when you're busted for something like that: "But it was so good!" It was actually pretty funny and fortuitous, because he was really taken with Lady Whistledown and wanted to know her identity. At that time, I had no idea and hadn't spent much time thinking about it, which he couldn't understand, as she was such a driving force for him in the narrative.

And that's how she came to be so critical. Originally, she was just fun and snarky and a way for me to telegraph information to readers quickly and easily, but she's come to represent so much more: the power of gossip and story, the way women developed agency in a restrictive society through manipulating what was seen and reported, and also the power of female writers to make their own living.

BETSY: It's really fun to speculate about the moment when Penelope Featherington decided to risk it all and pick up her pen, find a printing press, and scale a business operation where she'd quickly have the most power in the ton. Did she consider it for long, or was it a rash decision? Was it a response to an understanding that she might need a source of income because of her father? And once she was off to the presses, did she have any regrets? What's clear is that it's an unparalleled power move that carries a tremendous amount of risk, though apparently, as someone who feels marginalized and unseen by society, she felt it was a risk worth taking. Maybe seasons to come will tell.

Lady Whistledo
SOCIETY PAP

EXTRAORDINARY PEOPLE. EXTRAO

GAMBLING FOR GOSSIP?

Dearest reader, a question... Is anything more exhilarating than taking a gamble? For it is often the highest risk that carries the greatest reward. Yet, wager wrongly - and you might find yourself left with nothing but regret. Of course, one can never know for sure whether a wager will make a fortune, or ruin it. Unless, one chooses more secure pursuits... But we all know that nothing is more exciting than trusting your gut and taking a chance.

But, as the season continues, the biggest gamblers have yet to truly show their hand. Which leaves gossip in short supply in recent days. In fact, this author can think of no other event that merits a mention. So we shall all have to sit back and wait for them to show their hand. Or get planning on the next big social event which is bound to stir up some news notable of permanent black ink.

It is worthy of note, however, that the Duke and Duchess of Hastings have yet to entertain callers together. Our newlyweds are no doubt still secluded in nuptial bliss.

of excitement
the more obse
attended the
to notice tha
works hold s
newer towns
a heavy c
certain lad
attended
case she
figure pa
striking r
course th
thought
seem...
certain
countr
not ge
Blyth
seen

Sea
Also
are
Gr
w

JESS BROWNELL: In the writers' room, whenever you received a Lady Whistledown assignment, you knew that it would take some time because Whistledown has to add something—she doesn't merely comment on what we've already seen.

She is smarter, wittier, and more insightful than everyone else, and she's almost always armed with some type of metaphor, typically one that goes the extra step of reflecting the Regency era. The metaphor needed to be a comment on all the stories.

We had a narrow target to hit: flowery, biting, and sharp—an observation that could be applied to Simon and Daphne, or Colin, or really any of the players on the screen. One example is the moment after Daphne discovers how babies are really made and gets on top of Simon in that very controversial moment, which we paired with Marina's pregnancy news dropping. Lady Whistledown's voiceover in that moment could be applied to either woman.

> LADY WHISTLEDOWN (V.O.)
> Desperate times may call for desperate measures, but I would wager many will think her actions beyond the pale...

SHONDA: The books wait to reveal Lady Whistledown's identity until later—and originally, we were going to wait a beat as well. In fact, we had a whole other scene that we filmed as a red herring:

> --Who should step out of this carriage, wearing the same CLOAK we saw her wearing at the printing press, but... *CRESSIDA COWPER??!!*
>
> LADY WHISTLEDOWN (V.O.) (CONT'D)
> *Lady Whistledown.*

As the camera pans up from Lady Whistledown's cloak, it's Cressida Cowper's face that you see. But when we were staring at the cut, it just wasn't as interesting—we wanted to see Penelope's face, to bring the viewer in on the secret a bit earlier. By revealing it at the end of the first season—well before the ton finds out—it provided us with so much possibility for storytelling going forward. In Season 2, we get to know something that nobody else knows. It felt like if we waited, we would lose the opportunity to enjoy the secret.

SHONDA ON JULIE ANDREWS:

When Julie Andrews said she would do the voice of Lady Whistledown for us, I lost my mind. Before we made the ask, we worked so hard on her scripts to really nail the quality and make them elevated and perfect—you cannot have Julie Andrews as Lady Whistledown and not do the finest job possible. That said, I was joking that I couldn't imagine Julie Andrews saying some of these curse words. In my mind, she will always be Mary Poppins.

We are so grateful that she agreed to do it. I know Dame Julie Andrews because my second film was *Princess Diaries 2,* which she was in, but I made someone else ask her, because I assumed she was far too busy for us, and I didn't think I could handle the rejection. When she said yes, I was elated. I might have cried tears of joy when I first heard her voice over the film.

JULIE ANDREWS ON VOICING LADY WHISTLEDOWN:

I was delighted when Shonda Rhimes invited me to join the *Bridgerton* family. I've long been an admirer of Shonda's work, and this appeared to be a delicious project on a variety of levels. Initially, distance was a concern. Because Lady Whistledown is the narrator and never actually appears on screen, my work is entirely done via voice-over recording. This meant I was never able to meet any of my fellow company members in person, but Zoom calls helped and eventually scripts came in ahead of recording times which allowed me to digest and think about my character.

Finding Lady Whistledown's voice was my first priority. It was complicated in that I knew her true identity from the beginning but viewers of the show had to wait until the final episode of the first season to find out for themselves. I knew the character should sound upper class, considering that she self-publishes her weekly pamphlets that everyone reads so avidly. And although audiences now know that our talented purveyor of gossip is actually a young girl, the townspeople in the story still have no idea, and would likely assume the writer to be mature. So mature is what I aimed for. It's ironic that the characters in the film only *read* Lady Whistledown's words, whereas viewers of the show only *hear* them.

Initially, I narrated to film that had already been edited—just adding my voice over the story, so to speak—but it proved to be extremely challenging since my words had to fit exactly into the timing of every edited scene, and I had no space for expansion or subtlety. Subsequently, I have been able to pre-record tracks in my own rhythm and to my surprise, they have been well received and little else has been required.

Before every taping I repeat to myself the phrase, "My name is Lady Whistledown . . ." which are the very first words I recorded for the role. Finding that voice I am able to work my way back to the correct cadence for each episode. In real life I speak rather quickly, but for this narration, I discovered that I had to apply the brakes and make sure that each word was delivered succinctly, not just to be heard but to help convey to readers of my pamphlets the clarity and weight of my written words.

Not long after we began taping the first season, the COVID epidemic hit hard and going into a recording studio became impossible. Miraculously, I was saved by my eldest grandson, Sam. He lives near me and just happens to be a fine recording engineer. In very short order, he fashioned a tiny recording studio out of one of my guest room closets. Padding for sound consists of blankets, throws, and several pillows. Between Sam's equipment and Zoom calls connecting me with engineers and the production team in faraway places, I have managed to continue Lady Whistledown's journey while remaining comfortably in my own residence.

Sam and I have a great time recording together. We giggle about the bizarre invention of it all, but I delight in the odd circumstances that allow Grandmum and Grandson to work side by side—while having an absolute ball.

CHRIS VAN DUSEN: We recorded all of Julie's voice-over after we wrapped filming Season 1, and because it was in the midst of the pandemic, we did it all remotely. She was in a studio on Long Island, and Tom Verica and I were in Los Angeles on Zoom.

TOM VERICA: Julie Andrews Zoomed in to voice Lady Whistledown while we were cutting the episodes together. There aren't too many people whom I find intimidating, in that "Wow, that is so-and-so," but Julie Andrews is iconic, and she has that presence. She also has a tremendous sense of humor, and she had a lot of fun with what we asked her to do. She was also very frank with her opinions, which was very refreshing.

Instead of just reading the page, she always wanted to understand the context, and so I would walk her through the scenes and episodes and what had happened and what was at stake. She was very interested in what was happening in that moment and what we were looking for—she really wanted to bring the most out of both the script and the character.

LOVE? One has also heard through society chatter that Lord James Massing and Miss Cornish are courting and one truly hopes they are soon to be engaged. Of course they are truly an unlikely match, however once you see them together you are sure to be convinced of their love.' Twas only last week when even this author was convinced this relationship match would never see the light of this week, and that both Lord James Massing and Miss Cornish were acting on their own agendas. As we all know Miss Cornish has youth and beauty on her side in her first season and who is to question who she is yet to receive? Lord James Massing has seen many seasons pass, none with more promise than this. He is probably one of the most intriguing matches and has inherited, from his family, a vast expanse of acreage to go with his country estate. What more could a girl want? Seemingly she is yet to be bold over by Lord James Massing advances and they are seemly a perfect pair. We shall see what develops in the coming weeks and the most intrigue and speculation. Known for her courageous fashion choices and magnificent dinner parties, even Mrs Apsted may have outdone herself. As we all know Mr Apsted sadly departed many years ago and since then Mrs Apsted has become increasingly more social and has a vast amount of friends, some of which have questionable pasts. Anyway, whilst the party was in full spirit and dinner had been served, Mrs Apsted and one of her new friends were spotted sitting alone together in the garden – away from the party. Of course they may have just been taking an innocent breath of refreshing air, but considering this is not the first time the two have been seen alone together – one can only speculate.

—Chris Van Dusen

LAST WEEKS HIGH FASHION: Last Thursday eve, Mrs Arrowcroft hosted a splendid ball at her wonderfully decadent home on Grosvenor Street. It was attended by Mr and Mrs Dempsey, Misses Bray and Mrs Fergusson. This has been Mrs Wilkinson's first public appearance since her late husbands passing, nearing 10 months ago. She was dressed in delicate black lace, but aloud herself some colour through her accessories, for example her exquisite deep blue purse encrusted with gems – believed to be one of the last gifts from her last husband. Mrs Fergusson was dressed in a peach gown with a scolloped hem, cream gloves with a lace trim, which matched Mrs Fergusson's shawl perfectly. Tiny flowers had been french plated into her hair which suitably completed her look. As the guests arrived at Mrs Arrowcroft's home they were greeted with the magical music of her six piece string orchestra. Dancing commenced shortly after ten o'clock with everyone in full attendance, the couples took to the floor with enthusiasm and youth. By one o'clock a most sumptuous banquet was served and the guests commenced dancing soon after it was finished, keeping up the correct amount of spirit until a late hour.

Mr and Mrs Dempsey retired at two o'clock, Mrs Wilkinson and Mrs Fergusson were both escorted to and from the ball by their servants.

Mrs Lowe's last ball, the previous Wednesday, was one of the most intrigue and speculation. Known for her courageous fashion choices and magnificent dinner parties, even Mrs Lowe may have outdone herself this time. As we all know Mr Lowe sadly departed many years ago and since then Mrs Lowe has become increasingly more social and from that, has a vast amount of friends, some of which have questionable pasts. Anyway, whilst the party was in full spirit and dinner had been served, Mrs Lowe and one of her new friends were spotted sitting alone together in the garden – away from the party. Of course they may have just been taking an innocent breath of refreshing air, but considering this is not the first time the two

have been seen alone together - one can only speculate.

There shall forever be just two words that come to this author's mind the morning after any good party: Shock. And delight.

WEEKLY EVENTS: there are a lot of Balls debutantes to work on

Miss Sarah Mulberger and Mrs Harris's Ann Tuesday, Ms Claire M spectacular, Whitdon Grand Ball, Pope S Gordon's Annual Ball, Robert, Grand Supp Kelly Valentine Henr Avenue, Friday - Mr Seasonal Ball, Saltmar ball, Menton Road, Sa Hall, Edge Park Avenue

Ring Out The Bel society chatter that Lord James Massing courting and one tr to be engaged. Of cou match, however once convinced of when even this author match would never se Lord James Mass acting on their own Cornish has youth and her first season and w she is yet to receive? many seasons pass, no He is probably one of t and has inherited, fro acreage to go with his a girl want? Seemingly to be bold over by Lo they are seemly a p develops in the coming most intrigue and courageous fashion c parties, even Mrs Ap this time. As we all k many years ago and sin increasingly more soc amount of friends, so pasts. Anyway, whilst dinner had been serve new friends were spot garden – away from have just been taking air, but considering th have been seen alone t

FASHIONABLE THE WEEK: This are a lot of Balls an debutantes to work o

Monday - Miss Sar Square, Mr and Mrs H Avenue

Tuesday - Ms Claire N spectacular, Whitdon Grand Ball, Pope Squar

Wednesday - Mr T Gordon's Annual Ball, Forbridge Street, Robert, Baron Bownden's Grand Supper, Mare Rise

Thursday - Miss Kelly Valentine Hendry's Afternoon Tea, Sunday Avenue.

Friday - Mr David Crewdson's Spectacular Seasonal Ball, Saltmarsh Street, Miss Tally Kopacio's Ball, Menton Road. Saturday - Mr and Mrs Robinson's Ball, Edge Park Avenue.

RECENT NEWS:

Miss Cerrington has recently returned to her family i London after her extended stay in the country apparently with extended family. Mr and Mrs Voel

expect our Duchess will have a very carefully chosen guest list to ensure no more of her guests sordid secrets come to the surface and she knows to to keep her husband close, so theoretically it should all go smoothly. However, naturally one must always be carful who they let through their door as you never know what information they could carry out with them. So, we shall wait with baited breath to see what emerges from tonights soiree. Miss Cerrington has recently returned to her family in London after her extended stay in the country apparently with extended family. Mr and Mrs

"Lady Whistledown allowed us to explore the power of the written word. She is our one-woman Regency tabloid, and we get to see how she shifts public opinion and changes the narrative, just as social media does today."

have been seen alone together - one can only speculate

There shall forever be just two words that come to this author's mind the morning after any good party. Shock. And delight.

RECENT NEWS:

Miss Cerrington has recently returned to her family in London after her extended stay in the country apparently with extended family. Mr and Mrs Vosier arrived at their house late yesterday evening after

Vosier arrived at their house late after a short tour around Dorse preparations in their home for the Mrs Hooperwood had returned was on a visit to Mrs Eckingham these sorts of t For those re of how li st ask, is the of bettering ections of bot e the sort of household o morning. This ghts soiree do who has organ ts of the se th's previous osed sordid m standing figu a stop after illness after g a lot of dy. Of cour e country and e. However, g since beer ed Duke wil one other th with baited ghts soiree. Of sorts of th For those re of how st ask, is the of bettering ections of bo e the sort c household o morning. This ghts soiree do who has organ ts of the se th's previou sed sordid f standing figu will be slov her than his

Wednesday - Mr T. Gordon's Annual Ball, Forbridge Street. Robert, Baron Hownden's Grand Supper, More Rise.

Thursday - Miss Kelly Valentine Hendry's Afternoon Tea, Sunday Avenue.

Friday - Mr David Crewdson's Spectacular Seasonal Ball, Solmorch Street. Miss Tally Kapadia's Ball, Merton Road. Saturday - Mr and Mrs Robinson's Ball, Edge Park Avenue

expect our Duchess will have a very carefully chosen guest list to ensure no more of her guests sordid secrets come to the surface and she knows to to keep her husband close, so theoretically it should all go smoothly. However, naturally one must always be carful who they let through their door as you never know what information they could carry out with them. So, we shall wait with baited breath to see what emerges from tonights soiree. Miss Cerrington has recently returned to her family in London after her extended stay in the country apparently with extended family. Mr and Mrs

The Power of Gossip

DR. HANNAH GREIG ON THE HISTORICAL PRECEDENT OF LADY WHISTLEDOWN:

Julia Quinn talks about creating Lady Whistledown as a literary device, a means for front-loading information in the *Bridgerton* series, but choosing her as the narrator was also a [brilliant and] historically appropriate decision, for there was plenty of gossip printed in Regency London—the concept first emerged in the 1770s.

There are Regency pamphlets similar to Lady Whistledown's paper that survive in libraries today, and within them you can read about the private lives of the most public citizens—they truly pierced the reputations of this world of fashionable London; they revealed what had previously been hidden behind closed doors. People's daily activities were recorded and remarked on as a source of entertainment and conversation in a way we very much recognize today.

We often do not know exactly who wrote the original scandal sheets. Many were written under a pseudonym. But we have plenty of evidence that women, and often titled or aristocratic women like Penelope, were authors of these and many other printed works of the time. The most significant difference between the *Whistledown Papers* and the real scandal sheets of the time is the use of full names (a point that Quinn also makes clear). Historically, these would just use initials or other descriptions to indicate the subject, never a full name, to get around libel and defamation laws. The clues were easy to solve, though. Anyone keeping up with the comings and goings of fashionable society would have known who was being written about.

Gossip writing was risky for women but exciting, too, because it was an opportunity to have a real business—much like you'd buy a newspaper or a magazine, you would have paid for your gossip. Lady Whistledown was based on Mrs. Crackenthorpe, the pseudonymous writer of the *Female Tatler*, which was a gossip's guide to London in the 1710s. Crackenthorpe's real identity is not known, though there's certainly a lot of speculation.

It would be wrong, though, to suggest that writing scandal sheets and gossip offered a path to riches in Regency London. As today, it was hard to make a living at writing, even if you penned a bestseller. But even if money was uncertain, writing offered power: As the adage goes, the pen is sometimes mightier than the sword. People's reputations were made or broken and destinies were determined by what was printed. We see this throughout the *Bridgerton* novels and the show, in the ways in which Violet, Lady Danbury, Simon, and Daphne all manipulate Lady Whistledown to "see" and report what they want.

After all, it didn't take all that much to get tongues wagging. I think the basis of scandal is fairly continuous throughout history. You could say that it wouldn't be scandalous to be alone in the garden with the Duke of Hastings today, but people are still interested when two hot young celebrities are spotted together—there will always be speculation to follow about their relationship and what they're doing. As much as things change, some things stay the same!

"Bridgerton was not just a regular show—it's not like any other show ever made, in fact. We had to create and design a completely different world, to reimagine the Regency period in a way it's never been seen before. Shondaland did not want a history lesson; they wanted something new."

—Ellen Mirojnick, Costume Designer

HIRING THE WORLD

Critical Early Decisions

BETSY BEERS: Initially, it was probably difficult for Netflix to understand why we were spending so much money on the costumes. But we felt, very strongly, that we were creating a wholesale new look and feel for a period that we would never be able to find in Europe's costume houses, and we wanted it to be a bright, technicolor world, which we knew we couldn't find. Ultimately, we told them that the costumes were worth it for us, and that we would find other ways to be thrifty—but we felt we needed to spend on the visuals, that they would be critical in holding the world together.

Ellen Mirojnick is the first person we hired: She's a friend, and we had worked with her on our shows several times, and we knew she would nail period in a really fresh way. She helped Chris establish a palette and articulate the way we saw the world, particularly with its touches of modernity. We wanted to be sure that subconsciously, you would watch the show and perceive it as Regency, but you would instinctively feel that there was something incredibly relevant and current about it. You might not be able to put your finger on it, but it's there—you see it in the little haute couture Chanel-esque jacket, or the dress that you'd want to wear now.

So whether it was the costumes, the sets, the stage directions, or the music, there's this through line where there are not so subtle nods to current culture. It feels both relatable and escapist, and this vision was really achieved by every single part of production.

BRING ON THE BLING!

DR. HANNAH GREIG ON THE EXCESSES OF REGENCY ENGLAND

There was a culture throughout Europe of all the leaders—including Napoleon over in France—trying to out-glamour each other. If something could be gilded with diamonds—swords, staffs—they were doing it. If there were exotic goods and fabrics to be acquired, they wanted to be the first to have them. You hear a small reference to this tendency in *Bridgerton*, when George III and Queen Charlotte, during his brief period of lucidity, are talking about the kangaroos that they once imported.

In 1821, after his father died, George IV—son of our beloved Queen Charlotte—had an incredibly ostentatious coronation, which cost £230,000, which is the equivalent today of £115,000,000. He had a new crown made with twelve thousand diamonds. He built fancy grand palaces and acquired a tremendous amount of art, gold, and diamonds.

Well, the excess wasn't relegated only to royalty: Throughout high society, people were spending in a competitive way. This also paved the way for the Victorian period fifty to sixty years later, which was very, very different and almost a direct response to Regency England. That was a period marked by austerity, an aversion for scandal, and being buttoned up about everything.

COSTUME DESIGNER ELLEN MIROJNICK:

As the first ones on the production, our team was tasked with establishing the show's sensibility and palette, which was so exciting. Chris Van Dusen wanted a bonnetless universe: a seductive, inspirational, aspirational, and imaginative romantic fantasy that would connect with a modern audience. *Bridgerton* was not going to be like any other show we'd ever made. Shondaland did not want a history lesson; they wanted something new.

We did extensive research on the period to understand which elements we wanted to pull forward, whether it was the palette, fabrication, embellishment, or silhouette. We knew we needed many nods to Regency even as we made a world that any person would want to be part of. My greatest task was to take the period concept and turn it on its head—not to bastardize the Regency period but to enhance it.

We didn't have finished scripts when we started, but we had a basic outline of what was ahead of us. First things first: We assembled a world-class team, which took about a month. Because we were inventing an entirely new look for the period, we had to build everything. *Everything.* Thankfully, I had John Glaser, John Norster, and Ken Crouch on board, all of whom brought structure to the group and helped to facilitate the work ahead.

We had a person solely responsible for securing the fabric we needed, which was truckloads! We went to every single resource in New York, London, Florence, Rome, Madrid, shopping all over the world for the finest couture fabrics. We needed silks, satins, jacquards, and embroideries—an entire world of options. We looked for base fabrics, fancy fabrics, sparkly fabrics, and unusual fabrics.

Waiting in our London factory, we had extraordinary cutters, embroiderers, and appliqué people. They took what we bought and layered it together into entirely new fabrics. It was so fun to break the rules, and it was also remarkable how quickly we all adapted. The ladies we worked with are exquisitely talented at period—they know every element that goes into an historical garment—and I was asking them to throw it all away and go for something different. Honestly, we didn't know how it was going to work out. We knew that it would be either fantastic or a disaster. I'm pretty thrilled that it was the former.

Betsy Beers on Locating— and Building the World

One of the first steps of production was to figure out our locations; the fantasy being, of course, to film as much in London as possible while still accessing these amazing country estates. We looked at locations all over the country before deciding to film a good chunk of our location work in Bath for Season 1, because it's very well-preserved when it comes to Regency architecture.

The biggest puzzle piece, which our Season 1 producer Sarada McDermott sketched out for us, is that there are many beautiful locations, but they are not in the same areas. We looked at Liverpool, we looked at Greenwich, we honestly looked everywhere, but when it came down to the logistics of transporting our massive cast and crew all over England, we needed to narrow it down to a few zones. And then

we needed locations that we could build off of, because there are a lot of scenes that happen tangential to locations, like the Dark Walk in Season 1, or the garden terrace with Daphne and Simon. It was a puzzle, through and through.

When we hired Will Hughes-Jones, we knew we needed the right person aesthetically, but we also wanted someone who is naturally incredibly inventive, because we needed to capture the scope and breadth of the world without breaking the bank—or breaking everyone's backs traversing the whole of England. Once we narrowed down the locations, we focused on how best to use and maximize each one.

For the Bridgertons, we needed a space that is grand and beautiful but also very warm, where you instantly feel like you're in the home of a very happy family. We really wanted the image of all of these children tumbling down the stairs. In one of Charles Dickens's books, there's the line, "They weren't raised, they tumbled up," and I've never forgotten that. It's the idea of a lot of kids running around, that delightful and enjoyable chaos. That's how we opened the entire seasons. We juxtaposed that against the Featherington entryway, which is much more crafted. It's more aspirational, not at all focused on comfort or coziness.

We also thought a lot about the dining rooms, because we have those wonderful family dinners that telegraph exactly who the Bridgerton family is—passing dishes, throwing peas, a high Benedict in Season 2. We did that intentionally to contrast against Daphne and Simon in Hastings, when they're seated hundreds of feet away from each other, or the tone of the dinner with Mary's mother and father in Season 2. The dining room felt critical: The way each family is reflected in those rooms was a critical part of our storytelling.

**PRODUCTION DESIGNER
WILL HUGHES-JONES:**

When I was first approached about *Bridg-erton*, my call with Chris Van Dusen, Sara Fischer, and Betsy Beers was on Zoom—it was a new thing, and it was so strange to be interviewed that way. Normally, I'd sit next to someone and take them through mood-boards. During that conversation, I gleaned from Chris what the project was and what it wasn't—namely that it wasn't a typical period show. I told him I didn't think I had my moodboards quite right and asked for an hour to do a few more. I whipped some additional boards up, emailed them over, and ten minutes later, I got a call from the producer Sarada McDermott telling me I had nailed it and that they'd love for me to do it.

From there on out, it became a massive roller coaster. I don't think any of us realized what we were undertaking. If we had known, it would have scared a lot of people off! Honestly, if I had known how many flowers were involved, I would have thought twice about it. And balls. I really wasn't ready for the number of balls, flowers, and crazy cakes we'd need to do. When you walk into our prop store and see the sheer volume of artificial flowers we have, it's staggering.

BETSY: We also needed to animate this Regency world where people held themselves in an entirely different way and also spent a majority of their social hours dancing—Jack Murphy, our movement director, was extraordinary in realizing this period in very subtly modern ways.

CHOREOGRAPHER JACK MURPHY: In April 2019, I met with Betsy, Chris, Sara, Sarada, and Julie Anne Robinson at the Bloomsbury Hotel. Julie Anne said to me, "Pretend I don't know anything about Regency dance, how would you explain it to me?" And so I said, "Up you get," and pulled her to her feet, and we danced. It was wonderful. Chris wanted to know how I would modernize it, and so I took Julie Anne for another dance.

They knew exactly what they wanted. They were so clear, with incredible vision. There was no waste, no bluff, no sentimentality. I felt immediately that I had done a good interview, and I turned to Sarada, who escorted me out and said, "That was actually wonderful. If I don't get the job, it's actually fine, because that was nourishing." I knew if it was meant to happen, it would happen, that what is for you does not go by you. And so when I got the call ten days later from Sarada, I had almost forgotten about it. I had no attachment, because the interview itself was complete. I was gobsmacked when I got the job.

Julie Anne Robinson was an easy choice as our pilot director: She has worked with us for a long time, going all the way back to early seasons of *Grey's Anatomy.* She's delightful and great, and we've collectively had a long working relationship with her. We were also dealing with logistical issues we had not dealt with before, like . . . shooting a show in England while our little asses were in Los Angeles. And not only is Julie Anne Robinson incredibly talented in her own right, she is British. She knows the world, the land, and how to operate. Because not only are there cultural differences, the teams work in technically different ways and sets are managed differently—for example, there's no overtime in Britain.

But perhaps most importantly, Julie Anne Robinson is one of the only people we've encountered who is equally adept at comedy and drama. She really, really ticked all the boxes. So I convinced her to do it—I made it sound very appealing and very easy!—and then Chris, Alison, Shonda, and I had a long chat with her about how she would lay out the world.

Thankfully, we had a group of incredibly patient British actors who were willing to do locations all at once before doing their interiors when the roof caved in. And thankfully, Julie Anne was also incredibly patient, because directors are used to *finishing their episodes* before moving on to the next. But Julie Anne just went with it. And while yes, we asked her to do Episode Six to let the costume team catch up instead of doing Episode Two, which would have been typical, we really liked the idea of her doing it since there was so much intimacy: It felt important that the actors be able to work with someone with whom they were already comfortable rather than starting fresh with a new director.

DIRECTOR JULIE ANNE ROBINSON:
The way it works in television is the director who does the pilot sets the template and tone for the entire series. I love making pilots, that is my specialty. You get to make so many key decisions: You decide what music will be used in the dancing, the energy of the actors, the look of the show.

The theory is that you formalize the show, though with Shondaland, everyone is given a lot of latitude. There are some things that won't change, like costumes and sets, but it was all established very collabora-

"When Shondaland approached me about Bridgerton, *I wasn't looking to jump into something right away, as I had just come off a pilot and I was tired. But then Betsy called me and said, 'You should really look at this.' I adore Betsy, and so I caved and read the script. I have to say that my mom bought a new television to watch* Bridgerton, *and that it was her best friend's favorite show, who happens to be a nun in her eighties. So I stand by my decision."*

—Julie Anne Robinson

tively across teams: What will the hair and makeup be? What chair will we use? What color will be put on the walls? What is the style of the intimacy work? These are decisions that become very difficult to change in later episodes, even though every director treats their episode as a separate little movie. And when you watch, you can see every director's sensibility and style come through, though it still feels part of that main world that's been set up in the pilot.

The other upside of the pilot is that you get a lot longer run-up, because you're involved with all the preparation and planning for the show, including the preproduction. I think about it as a jigsaw puzzle that I'm putting together as I go. It's all in my head, or on paper, or in storyboards—and as I move forward, I hope I don't miss a critical piece. But the main thing is to go in with a plan. On a production of this scale and complexity, you are not winging it!

BETSY: I would be remiss without mentioning Tom Verica, a producing director who has a big umbrella role at Shondaland, overseeing the direction of all our shows—he is often the connective tissue who ensures that all the other directors have what they need to express their own creative vision while keeping a through line to the energy of the show.

DIRECTOR AND PRODUCER TOM VERICA:

I came into the first season of *Bridgerton* as a hired director, and somewhere in the midst of production, I had the opportunity to expand my position with Shondaland into an advisory role. I'm not sure that directing a romance novel is what I set out to do, exactly, but knowing Chris and Shonda and the team, and that I'd be diving into a completely foreign world—British actors in another country in a period piece—was very appealing. I felt rejuvenated by it in a lot of ways. I had directed *For the People* for Shondaland, and so Regé and I were already friends, which made it really easy. To see him in a different light, acting in London, was really exciting, and I think that came through on the screen.

When we came back for Season 2, I was in my official expanded position, working with all of the directors and staying in touch with all of the show prep. I became responsible for the totality of the project. In some ways, it's similar to what Chris does—he has his finger on the pulse story-wise, but I come in more from the visual and tone standpoint. We encourage all of our directors to bring their voice, but if something bumps and is outside the boundary, I can rein it back in. Chris and I worked closely to find the glue and create cohesiveness. And because of my shorthand with Shonda, I know what she likes and what's important—we have a telepathic connection of sorts. I can distill and articulate what she wants to whatever department needs to hear it, which is critical in keeping a show on the rails as it evolves.

*"As a casting director, you have an opportunity
to open the door and present a different perspective,
including one that might create a new narrative."*

—Casting Director Kelly Valentine Hendry

DEFINING "THE TON"

Casting

BETSY BEERS: At Shondaland, we have a tradition of introducing actors to the world. We're not as interested in a viewership that comes flooding in because they recognize somebody. So we were definitely not building the *Bridgerton* world around a specific marquee actor. Obviously, we wanted to cast the right people, but we also wanted to integrate—no pun intended—the story of, for example, Simon and Lady Danbury, and the concept of this hard-won title that could potentially be snatched away from you at any point, and how hard people fought to keep their standing in society. That felt very real and modern to us, but also relatable to that period of time. It became incredibly clear, at a particular point, that the world had to be color-conscious, not color-blind, and that it would be inclusive—which it probably actually was. There is so much erasure of history, which we're only starting to understand now. The amount of talent that never made the history books is staggering.

DR. HANNAH GREIG: Often when we look at the past, we only ask a specific set of questions—who was in power, who married whom, who had status or fame—and this is how vast swaths of people are excluded and erased from history. It's always important to remember that stories about the past are not straightforward or simple—they are complicated, rich, and complex. One example of this is that we've never seen people of color in a period drama, which has led us to believe that people of color didn't exist in Regency England. This is not true. We need to tell stories about the past that tell a fuller and more accurate version of the truth.

CASTING DIRECTOR KELLY VALENTINE HENDRY:

Shondaland gave us carte blanche as we began to imagine and assemble the cast, looking within every conceivable corner in terms of training and ability. Many of the cast members were new to audiences across the globe, but we know them from the theater here in the UK.

We saw hundreds of actors for the show and then ultimately presented between five to twelve options for each character. Some actors were cast straight from tape—like Nicola Coughlan and Claudia Jessie—whereas others came in to read, did chemistry tests, and so on. For a character like Daphne or Lady Featherington, who are at the center of so many dynamics and relationships, getting that casting right was critical.

The process was fascinating, too, because we didn't have full scripts—we could send actors a page or two of dialogue, and they needed to work from that to imagine the full spectrum of who this character was. Delivering against that is a feat, but there's also something really nice about not being too literal on the page. This allows actors to imagine the character without too many preconceived ideas about their arc.

One of the other prevailing Shondaland themes is that we only cast nice people. It sounds trite, but everyone on the cast is an incredibly hard worker who makes this ensemble even better. They are effectively an extended family who will be around for seasons—they have to really love each other.

"Chemistry is a big, fat, accidental win, if I'm honest."

—Kelly Valentine Hendry

The
MATRIARCHS

QUEEN CHARLOTTE

"I wish to be entertained."

SHONDA: I'm obsessed with Queen Charlotte—to a slightly unhealthy extent. In our *Bridgerton* world, she was the Beyoncé of the day: fierce, fabulous, unexpected, weird. She's a fascinating creature. In fact, I want to be like her, particularly with the wigs. I told our merchandising department that if they make the wigs, I'll wear one every day.

BETSY: I wouldn't blame you—except that they were so heavy! Never forget that Golda needed a leaning post on the side of the set so she could get the weight and pressure off her back. In some ways, those heavy wigs were the perfect metaphor for Queen Charlotte: an over-the-top presence, and yet she was suffering underneath. Seemingly so much freedom and power, and she was still double-corseted.

SHONDA: Exactly—and seeking fun and a break from her sadness through society scandal, dictating matches, making mischief, maneuvering via gossip, and the hunt for Lady Whistledown's identity. It's such an interesting balance. Here is a woman who has everything she could possibly want, and yet she's bored and her husband is disappearing into madness. What is she supposed to do with her time? She's a woman with weight, and tons and tons of power, who is also still in prison. She is in a golden cage.

BETSY: Historically, you often hear about the madness of King George, but you never hear about Queen Charlotte. That was such an interesting opportunity for us.

SHONDA: Even though she didn't appear in Julia Quinn's books, we made her a foun-

dational character in *Bridgerton*. While the queen is an archetype, a figurehead, she is not one-dimensional—she's not only the most powerful woman in the country but also one of the most complex, both behind the scenes, in her relationships, and in the way she shows up in the world. She is not only running Regency England but changing and informing it.

KELLY VALENTINE HENDRY: Historically, there is documentation that Queen Charlotte was mixed race—we were definitively going to cast a woman of color, which was very exciting, because in historical dramas, especially in the UK, this has never been done.

BETSY: We needed someone to play Queen Charlotte who has major impact. We knew getting the right queen was going to be really, really difficult, because we needed someone with an enormous presence. We needed an actor who would be fun to watch and also scary enough to be taken seriously.

SHONDA: We flipped when Golda was available and willing to do it. We loved her audition. And then we needed to make her larger than life. She's changing the course of society—she needed to be as big as you could possibly make her in terms of size. Some of the wigs were three, four, or five wigs put together; her dresses were enormous. She was delightful, she was glorious.

KELLY: Golda Rosheuvel was clearly Queen Charlotte from the minute she walked into the room—not surprising, because there is no one more fabulous than Golda. Sometimes when you read with actresses during auditions, you get a similar performance—people attack the role in the same way. But Golda was unique; her Queen Charlotte was her own invention, and that's what we see in *Bridgerton*. It's impossible to imagine Queen Charlotte in any other way.

GOLDA ON QUEEN CHARLOTTE: I felt so lucky that Queen Charlotte was written to be so well-rounded—she's not just about the fun, the glamour, the parties, the gossip, and the scandal. She is also coping with the loss of her husband to his mental illness—there is deep, meaningful truth to her.

This is important when it comes to representation. You get a character like Queen Charlotte, who exposes the beauty of humanity—that we are all, regardless of race and class, capable of suffering. That we are all capable of love, hatred, tears, joy,

frustration, and need. It's weird to say this, but *Bridgerton* shows that Black and brown people exist and love in the same way as white people—even when they're royal.

There is a hierarchy to this world, of course, but between all the women, there was a real bond that I hope was palpable—I hope the audience could feel that they were emotionally connected in a type of sisterhood within a society that was extremely limiting in how they could exert their power.

I built her character through my relationships with Lady Danbury, Violet, even Lady Featherington. I knew who she was in that context. I also felt like I knew Queen Charlotte, because for the first time in my career, I was channeling my mother. I'm biracial. My father was Black and Guyanese, and my mother was white and British. My mom was very posh and held her-

self beautifully. Before the war, she had a nanny and her family had butlers. My grandfather was the headmaster of a public school, which in England is what we call fancy private schools. So my mother was quite privileged, and in the role of Queen Charlotte, I was able to tap into her heritage and channeled her as this powerful, beautiful, generous matriarch. It was the first time I felt like I could really be her while acting. She passed away in 2020 and never got to see *Bridgerton*, but she saw me in costume as Queen Charlotte in pictures. I am very grateful for that, because she recognized herself in me and in the queen. My mother saw herself as part of a complicated heritage and family and culture—but also as doing something new and unexpected. She didn't make the typical choices, and neither did the queen.

LADY DANBURY

"Your regrets are denied."

SHONDA: Lady Danbury feels like the only free woman in the room—in a way, I think she really is.

BETSY: I love that recurring joke in the books, that you marry somebody and they do you the favor of dying—it sounds terrible, but in a way, that's what was required for liberation.

SHONDA: That's a powerful idea, that the only time a woman is free in Regency society is when the man she is attached to dies—that is an essential transition for her to recoup her money and power, and in some ways, women can't have love and power concurrently.

BETSY: It's one thing to recoup your power—but then another to wield it, which is also what makes Lady Danbury so fascinating to watch. She is a master of this game; she knows how to maneuver people to get what she wants, for them to do what she thinks they should do, but it somehow doesn't come across as manipulative.

SHONDA: Lady Danbury can see the whole board; she understands the importance of strategy because she's watched various people play out their hands. She misses nothing. And she's never loath to speak her mind.

BETSY: It's like that great line when Simon first eats with the Bridgerton family, and they're contemplating the identity of Lady Whistledown. Francesca is convinced that Lady Danbury must be Whistledown, and then Daphne reminds her sister that Lady Danbury has no need to hide behind a scandal sheet or hold her tongue.

SHONDA: "Lady Danbury quite enjoys sharing her insults with society directly. She would never bother herself writing them all down." That's a great moment—it also gets at Danbury's efficiency and the idea that she doesn't have to waste time with niceties. She has the privilege of being able to cut right to the chase—society can't punish her for stepping out of line.

ADJOA ANDOH: Lady Danbury is powerful, yes; and part of that power comes from the fact that she is now retired from a life where she needed to strategize for her own survival. Simon is somewhat of a surrogate son to her, but she is otherwise free to do as she pleases. That is a relative miracle. She uses this privilege in Season 2 to take the Sharmas under her wing as well, and to sponsor them for the season.

All of the other women, even Lady Bridgerton, are strategizing within the very narrow parameters of society. They are finding the angles, really needing to be elegant in the way that they box clever. This maneuvering looks pretty and romantic occasionally, and it is certainly entertaining, but the reality is that they are fighting for their lives—the limited choices these women can make within the confines of what Regency society offers will determine their future happiness. It is far from just being a game.

Lady Danbury understands this because she's lived it—and made it successfully to the other side—and accrued a lot of power in the process. But it was a careful waltz. I love that scene between Lady Danbury and Young Simon, for example, where she says, "You have a stammer now, how are you going to manage that in your life?" And then she explains to him, "I was fearful of things in my life, and so the way I overcame my fear was by putting my best self forward, my boldest, fiercest self forward. I made myself the most terrifying creature in any room I entered." I love that Lady Danbury, who seems to have such a thick veneer and be completely unfazed by life, shares that she, too, is not invincible. But she's built her armor and protected herself by making wise choices within society, and that's the true source of her power. How many of us do that in real life? We act strong, and that, in turn, creates strength.

KELLY VALENTINE HENDRY:
While you can argue that the casting of all the principals was hugely important, Lady Danbury is critical—in a way, she is the most massive matriarch, sort of the Maggie Smith of *Downton Abbey*. Yes, you should love her, but you should be right scared of her as well.

There was no color-blind casting, we were certain that Lady Danbury was a Black woman of a certain age and that she required an actor who could embody her fabulousness. So here in the United Kingdom, Adjoa Andoh is one of the theater's grande dames—not only is she a leading actress, but she's been at the forefront of women playing male roles, especially in Shakespeare.

We checked her availability, and I held my breath, because she is not available very often. When she came in to read, her first question was: "Kelly, why am I here?" She meant as a Black woman, a Black actress. I love that she asked the question, because the question needed to be asked.

ADJOA: As someone who has grown up in this country with the history of this country—you know, you can't try out for costume dramas, you can't go for historical romance. And so typically, actors of color think, "Oh, another job I won't get." I needed to know that this was an opportunity to be in it—and also that I was expected to be myself, a Black woman, not a Black woman pretending that she is white. I needed to know that the auditions weren't color-blind. Because when we say we're color-blind, whose color are we being blind to? I am the color I am. I delight in my race, and I wouldn't want to be anything else. I think I was born with a winning ticket, thank you very much.

Adjoa and Golda on Recognizing and Seeing Each Other On and Off the Screen

"As low as you can go, Lady Danbury?"

—Queen Charlotte

ADJOA: That little moment between the two of them always makes me laugh. These are two people who have a long-lived knowledge of each other—they share a sense of humor, and they know what their status is in the hierarchy. It's a bit like that moment between Queen Elizabeth and First Lady Michelle Obama when they ended up talking about how much their feet hurt. It's a social code between women, a shared identity—and the line about her curtsying captures it.

GOLDA: There are a lot of moments like that throughout *Bridgerton,* where the door kind of cracks open to the backstory and history of the characters. These two certainly have their own common language and a deep understanding of each other. They've seen it, and they've been it.

ADJOA: We know from Lady Danbury's flashback scenes with young Simon that she is carrying around a certain amount of fragility—and we get a sense of that from the queen as well, that she's really suffering. You have to believe that these two women, laden with status, use their salty tongues and senses of humor to lighten the load a bit.

GOLDA: They can certainly sniff out the people who are just speaking a load of nonsense.

ADJOA: They don't suffer fools gladly. I think they would have been very attractive to each other at a young age, that sense of a conspirator and companionship within society.

GOLDA: Our relationship in real life is quite like that as well. You know, I remember seeing you in the park sometimes, and you came up in the theater before me, and so I would just tip my hat to you. You'd be walking with your family, and we'd share a glance that said: "I see you, I know you."

ADJOA: When Queen Charlotte first arrived, Lady Danbury would have been established in the court. In actuality, Charlotte married the king the day she landed. She wouldn't have spoken the language or had a friend in the world, and so I'm sure she was searching for allies. Isn't it interesting to speculate on the practicalities of their friendship and what they would have communed about over the decades?

GOLDA: Absolutely. They have a long-lived experience of admiration and fondness for each other—with some salt and lemon juice thrown in there as well. They are naughty ladies, which is pretty fabulous as well.

LADY VIOLET BRIDGERTON

*"What I wanted, dearest, was for you to
have the best, not in terms of rank, but love."*

BETSY: We were really struck by this idea of a mother in Regency England who had lost her husband—a husband that she loved, maybe more than her kids—who had all of these children to marry off. But she's not driven by expediency or social climbing. The determinant for a good marriage, in her measure, is not wealth or status or dowry; she wants every single one of her children to marry for love. It's a radical idea for a woman in society at the time, an amazing sort of novelty. And Violet, of all people, knows that love comes with huge cost and risk—you can lose it all—but she still feels like it's the most important thing. I love that we get to see Violet go through this in Season 2 and yet still insist on this for her children.

SHONDA: I really like Violet. When she tells off her son Anthony, when she puts those children in their place, she is interesting—she's not a pushover, and she's also not pushy. It's such a delicate balance. And she seems to have a capacity, probably because she's experienced much love and grief, to really hold space for her kids—to let them erupt at her, attempt to steamroll her, to express their resentment at her—and yet she's nonplussed and never a victim. She is quietly fierce. I thought that scene between Daphne and Violet, where Daphne is yelling at Violet for not better preparing her for her wedding night and marriage, was fascinating, because you know that Violet's mother told her nothing. Having that talk

with her daughter was probably the boldest thing Violet ever had to do. Violet really did her very, very best—for her kids. And she does so with so much patience and grace.

BETSY: Yes. She is pulling strings, yet at no point is she dictating to Daphne, or any of her children, really, what they must do or the decisions they must make. She holds such a beautiful line of allowing her children autonomy while also ensuring they don't walk right off a cliff. She's a mother who is creating an environment where each child can grow into the best version of themselves.

RUTH GEMMELL: I auditioned using the scene where she's talking to Anthony in the study, after she's invited the duke to dinner. It's a fantastic scene because she really shows her strength, both pointing out a woman's lot in society while also instructing her son on the gaps in his own knowledge. I love that about Violet: She loves him and will let him believe that he's in charge, but really, she is in charge. She's had a lot of practice! She's had eight children!

LADY FEATHERINGTON

"Circumstances change, ladies. Sometimes overnight."

SHONDA: Lady Portia Featherington is one of the most compelling characters on the show—and also the most misunderstood. She's always doing "terrible things," but really, she's just working to ensure the survival of her family and their place within the social status using the only tools at her disposal. And she's also, incidentally, hilarious.

BETSY: She's so wonderful and ridiculous. And it would have been easy to leave her there, but her humanity is so beautifully expressed in Season 1 through her relationship with Marina. At first glance, it seems like she's being cruel, but in the scene where she takes Marina to a poor neighborhood, she's really just desperately trying to help Marina understand the system under which she is constrained and the game she needs to play in order to save herself. It seems callous at first glance, but this is the only way she knows how.

SHONDA: Precisely. And she is legitimately perplexed as to why Marina would choose to live in squalor rather than just pick a man, literally any man—and a man who might die soon, for good measure. For Lady Featherington, that is the only natural choice. What a man represents to her is not love, and it's not happiness, and it's not joy—it's shelter, food, and clothing. Lady Featherington is telling her that she may not love the car, but it's going to get her to where she needs to go.

BETSY: Well, she's certainly a survivor as much as she's a cautionary tale. She may have bought into the dream when she was young—that the right strategic marriage is all she needs—but she's all the wiser

because of it. And when her husband dies at the end of Season 1 and really puts her in a perilous place, you know she will find a way to survive. I loved her evolution in Season 2. We of course see how she carefully uses Jack's seductive behavior as the solution to her struggle to keep her station. That relief is countered by her epiphany that she's being asked to give up her daughters in exchange for filthy luchre. We find to our surprise that her heart is in the right place. I also thought it was delightful to see her get her ball. When the Queen arrives, she literally becomes a puddle in the middle of the scene. There's something wonderful about her triumph, particularly after two seasons of watching her enviously look on as the rest of the ton gets their balls.

"Lady Featherington could be played as a very dislikable, ugly, and stupid character, and yet, at the end of the day, you feel sorry for her. That is very hard to do—to take someone who is kind of despicable and make her someone who engenders sympathy. But Polly Walker is a genius, and she accomplishes this and wins the day. You know, you have to fall from a great height to become a hero, which Portia Featherington does. And she does it so beautifully in such hideous fabric. Actually, it was beautiful fabric, made a little hideous—a perfect metaphor for Portia."

—Kelly Valentine Hendry

POLLY WALKER ON PORTIA:

Lady Portia Featherington is a survivor, and she's also a relic of the time: She operates in a society where it is impossible for women to get any of their needs met outside of marriage—they have no social status without a man. I don't think she has ever known love; she doesn't have that luxury. Unlike Lady Bridgerton, who has wealth, security, and highly desirable children, Portia is swimming upstream.

She recognizes that she is on the brink of ruin, her husband is only a hindrance, and she really can't depend on anyone but herself. And Mrs. Varley: She is really her only intimate relationship, the only person in whom she confides and trusts.

She doesn't have time for sentimentality, softness, soothing nurturance. She is on the edge of a hysterical breakdown, on the precipice of social ruin, alienation, poverty. She's also a misfit, she's just a natural outlier. Yes, she's controversial and pushy and ambitious—and we don't like those qualities in women—but that's why I love her. She may not be Mother Teresa, but she does wear her heart on her sleeve, and you get the sense that she really, deeply cares—she's doing the best she can. But her affection is bound by the reality and practicality of their situation. She has no patience for romanticism. She's indomitable, and you know she will always pick herself back up after she's been knocked down. She is trying to pass this type of practicality of thinking down to her daughters.

Shonda on the Connections
Between the Characters

One of the things I love most about *Bridgerton* is that it is ultimately about agency and relationships. Relationships of all kinds. People want to focus on the romance, but the show is about so much more. There are amazing friendships between women—for instance, the relationship between Penelope and Eloise is so moving and funny and true. The pains they suffer are relatable for anyone. I also love the relationship between Lady Danbury and Queen Charlotte. And Violet and Lady Danbury, for that matter. These are powerful women moving the chess pieces of society and finding their way around one another. But my favorite relationships are the ones Violet has with her children. The tension between Violet and Anthony is brilliant, as is the bond between Violet and Daphne (who can forget the scene where Violet tries to explain sex and ends up talking about puppies?). The care that Violet shows as a mother toward each one of her children is what builds the bond we as the audience have with the Bridgerton family as a whole. I can't wait to see how it is further explored.

One relationship that I find haunting is the one between Queen Charlotte and King George. His mental illness has left him a shell of a man. And I love seeing the ways in which Charlotte has chosen to deal with that—which is to say, she has chosen none at all. Charlotte's choice to stay as oblivious as possible to this king is heartbreaking. You can see the pain in her face in those scenes. But it also allows you to understand why she throws herself into things that may seem frivolous to the rest of us—unearthing the identity of Lady Whistledown, meddling in the marriage mart. She has nothing else to focus on—or perhaps she's looking for a distraction.

Charlotte's backstory is fascinating and one we are looking forward to exploring in the prequel about her life.

PHOEBE DYNEVOR: On paper, Daphne isn't very relatable: She's the ideal debutante, kind, nice, lovely . . . she gets everything that she wants, she behaves perfectly. So how do you turn her into a complex human?

I wanted to give her a bit of anxiety as a mechanism for understanding her more. After all, our show may have been set in the 1800s, but there are still a lot of parallels to modern life today, particularly in the ways women are portrayed in the media or on social media. We have the same pressure to perform perfection. We have the same instincts now to build women up and then tear them down for sport.

In my mind, society doesn't really change—technology does. And so the tabloid sheets of Regency England are mirrored in Instagram today. One moment she's the diamond who can do no wrong; the next, she's failing in everyone's eyes. In many ways, Daphne refuses to let her fate be determined by other people's opinions, and so she determines to shape those opinions for them, to strategize with Simon to change the story. Her story changes quickly, but she manages to move even faster—I really admire that about her. I loved playing Daphne because she is, at heart, very empowered.

ANTHONY

"I fight for the family I have. And you will never understand because you were born to marry into another family while I was born to carry on the Bridgerton name. That is what outweighs anything else. It is rather easy to be selfish when you have no one else to whom you must answer."

BETSY: From the beginning of Season 1, Anthony struggles with the idea of what it means to be a responsible man of the house. He really makes a hash of things for Daphne, partly out of this idea that nobody is good enough for her, in the same way that nobody is good enough for him. He approaches it like he's doing a deal, not understanding what it is to create a loving marriage. Over the course of Season 2, we come to understand why he's so avoidant and scared of intimacy.

SHONDA: We really see this arc and early trauma of watching his dad die in front of him, his mother fall apart, and suddenly, he's thrust into a position of overwhelming responsibility. That birthing scene captured the entire idea: Violet at the mercy of her son who doesn't really know anything about anything.

BETSY: You get the sense that Violet missed her moment to really guide him into picking up this mantle. Clearly, there's some anger and frustration there for both of them—

that her boy is suddenly in charge, for one, that she lost her husband and position in the family at the same time. We really see Violet get through to him, and he starts to understand that his job is to create an environment where people can flourish—not force the flourishing.

SHONDA: It's hard for Anthony because his father is almost sainted. In his mind and, theoretically, everyone else's minds, he will always fall short—there's no way to match that legacy.

BETSY: Jonathan is such a great actor, and he really managed to telegraph the idea that you not only can't be your father, but you can't learn from your father, either, because he's not there. His experience taught him at a young age that you can lose the people you love—so falling in love is a scary thing to do.

JONATHAN BAILEY: I initially read for Simon—they sent me two scenes with Simon's lines, a scene with Daphne and one with Anthony. Then I met with Alison Eakle, Chris Van Dusen, and Betsy Beers, and we talked about everything relevant to the story and personal to each of us, and really got to know each other. Something was fizzing in a very confusing way!

But they asked me if I'd consider reading for Anthony and make a longer commitment. I was heading to Coachella, where I was planning to camp, which they thought was a wild and crazy British thing to do. They also told me the traffic would be terrible, so they sent me on my drive with three scripts loaded up on my iPad so I could get a sense of Anthony and whether I felt resonant with him.

I could see what Anthony was for Daphne's story, and how his character served a specific function, which is always very exciting. His actions wouldn't stand up in a modern court in terms of gender roles, but I was really drawn to him. Being the young-est in a big family, I liked the idea of being the eldest, and this sense of lineage. It felt like an interesting way to explore masculinity, and privilege, and the patriarchy—that all started popping in my mind.

I went to the music festival, finished my holiday, and then got the second book in the series so I could look into Anthony's future. I inhaled that book. That's when I realized how absurd it is that romance novels haven't been given a platform. The *Bridgerton* books, in particular, are these psychologically complicated stories about love and what it means—they are broad, interesting, and each sibling gets their own journey. It's a brilliant concept.

And Anthony, meanwhile, just gets better and better. It's a tragic, really awful story. There was so much to get into—this loss of his father along with the hopelessness and burden of responsibility he bears—and unravel and peel away. And then he gets to pass the baton to the next sibling. I love that concept. With *Bridgerton,* you play your character, as we all do—you get to be

the lead in your own life—and then you get to support others in interesting subplots.

One of the pleasures of playing Anthony is that I really get to share a story with my mom, Violet, and we go deeper and deeper every season. He was really abandoned by her in his grief, and his siblings weren't old enough to support him. In Season 1, you see how incredibly confused he is in the way he treats Siena. It was a brilliant way to show the toxicity—not at all excusing it—of the human condition that's been created by trauma and a society that puts pressure on young people when they're not ready. It's easy to understand why he's disillusioned. His idea of love at that point is completely off: He doesn't know how to live up to his dad's legacy, he doesn't know how to share

responsibility, and he doesn't know how to make himself vulnerable—and so he makes himself vulnerable, ironically.

There's no therapy in Regency London, otherwise he would have racked up a massive bill. But in the second season, he gets therapy in some ways: He's encouraged and sometimes forced to identify where things have gone wrong. He has to communicate. He has to find acceptance, weirdly, that he's actually better and more worthy than he's believed himself to be. We start to see an acceptance, and the fascinating thing is that it would only have come from meeting Kate. Anthony doesn't get there through his own work—he gets there because he meets the right people and is forced to face the ghosts of his past.

Bridgerton Brothers

"So much of Benedict is exploring himself as a reflection of Anthony, because when you're talking to your brother, in some way you are talking to aspects of yourself. It makes these relationships very tricky. And in Season 2, as Anthony is finding himself and finding love, Benedict is very much his companion in that, even though he might not be the companion Anthony necessarily wants simply because they're very different. But they inform each other's journeys in really interesting ways."

—Luke Thompson

"I think Colin probably spent a lot of time trying to pick everyone's spirits up during these harder times. You see this in him now, and also how he is generally unfazed by all the drama unfolding in the family—he's pretty disengaged. I think that is part of his coping mechanism due to losing his dad when he was so young and understanding it's better to steer a wide path through the hard stuff than take it on."

—Luke Newton

"I think Anthony has a fair amount of resentment toward the other siblings because they didn't experience the trauma of their father's death to the same extent: He was really alone, separated from the rest of us, because he was suddenly the man of the house—and our mother wasn't there for him."

—Jonathan Bailey

BENEDICT

"Things may seem bleak now, brother. But if I am learning anything from my art studies, it's that it is almost always a matter of perspective. I look at my art, and if I do not like what I see, I may alter the color palette, but I certainly do not toss the entire design aside. Perhaps you, too, could do the same in your own life."

BETSY: Benedict is the best. On one hand, it would be so hard to have a brother like Anthony, and on the other hand, it would be so easy to have a brother like Anthony. In that period, the older son inherits the title and land and responsibility and has to become the man of the house, letting all the brothers off the hook. It doesn't seem like Benedict really minds . . . at all.

SHONDA: Certainly not, he is thrilled! There's that great moment in Season 1 before the duel, when you watch Benedict's face drop at the prospect of Anthony getting shot. I'm sure he'd mourn his brother, but the real tragedy would be having to pick up the mantle and give up the artist's den.

BETSY: In many ways, Anthony's fate is inescapable—there's no way that he can shrug off his responsibility. But when you're not the oldest, you have to figure out what you want to be when you grow up. Benedict's path is totally relatable to modern audiences. You have this incredibly strong, driven, articulate older brother who, either by desire or family responsibility, has to carry the burden.

SHONDA: You can't imagine Benedict carrying the burden, it's so contrary to his personality. He just wants to have fun, and drink, and play with beautiful women, and paint. But he's lovely about it, really, he's not a rake—I think this is because he's not disobeying anyone's expectations by following his passion and his heart.

BETSY: Benedict doesn't want to be Anthony at all. Benedict just wants to know what Benedict wants. In Season 1, he discovers the space to try and figure out who he wants to be, which is to not be a traditional Bridgerton. And Eloise really pushes him on that path, since he has freedom to explore in a way that is blocked to her.

SHONDA: Yes, and while he might like to paint, he's really most attracted to the freedom and the exuberance of expression. I don't know that it's about earning his spot as a great painter as much as it seems to be the most fun and interesting profession on offer.

BETSY: In Season 2, he wants to figure out a way to express himself, and art presents itself as that way. We really see his journey. I love that moment when he discovers Anthony paid his way in, and Eloise is effectively like, "Who cares?"

SHONDA: Yes, who cares. Because it's not so much about his talent as it is about applying himself to something—and something that liberates him rather than stultifies him.

LUKE THOMPSON: There is something at the center of Benedict that's confused, because he has creative instincts. I think the challenge for anyone who has those instincts is that you oscillate between thinking you're a piece of shit, and that everything you create is rubbish, and then you go the other way and think, "Oh my God, I am a *genius*!" Obviously, neither of those is true. And so part of Benedict's jour-

ney is to stop shifting between thinking he's either brilliant or terrible and to really find his place within that spectrum.

The big thing for Benedict is finding himself outside of his family. He's really navigating something that is his alone—his own path in the world. There are eight Bridgerton kids, and they are all a bit similar, forged from the same stuff in different combination. There's a wonderful line in the *Bridgerton* book that's Benedict's story, where Julia Quinn writes, "Benedict was a Bridgerton, and while there was no family to which he'd rather belong, he sometimes wished he were considered a little less a Bridgerton and a little more himself." That really nails it. As Benedict, I'm a member of this family, but who else am I? It's exciting to be someone who doesn't know exactly who he is.

"I also loved the use of the bee—I don't know if that was a moment of genius from Ellen Mirojnick or Will Hughes-Jones, but hey both picked it up and used it throughout the show. It was these tiny details that made the world feel complete."

—Betsy Beers

COLIN

"Our relationship has taken shape so naturally over the years, one could take it for granted. You have always been so constant and loyal, Pen."

BETSY: It is no coincidence that both Simon and Colin are travelers—they are literally and figuratively looking for their place in the world. Colin is a curious person, and I think he feels that his answers are out there somewhere, which is why you sense this pushing and pulling and, ultimately, confusion. He's in a tough spot, being the third son. In a world where you only need an heir and a spare, Colin doesn't know where he fits—and he's constantly looking to transform himself.

SHONDA: Yes, he wants to make his mark. And he hopes that the world will inform him of how to do this, or at least show him the way. Instead, he keeps finding himself trying to save women—that's his instinct, he thinks that's what will deliver his purpose.

BETSY: Yes, he wants to be a savior, to be gallant. I don't know if that's a reverberation from being too young to do anything to help his dad or his mom, but he has a strong instinct to rescue the damsel in distress. You can really see his chest swell when he rescues the Featheringtons. What do you think that's about?

SHONDA: He really is in love with the idea of doing the right thing more than the thing itself. But I do love him for it, this fixation on honor. I think it's very interesting.

BETSY: Yep. There's also something really poetic about the fact that his heroics are always in secret—he is saving the Featheringtons, but that feat depends on nobody ever finding out about it.

SHONDA: Yet that's a central theme of *Bridgerton:* There are no secrets in the ton.

LUKE NEWTON: I think we all auditioned for the duke—the scene where the duke is promenading with Daphne. Then I auditioned for Colin. That's when I really started to fall in love with the project. I came in for a final interview with Chris Van Dusen, Julie Anne Robinson, and Betsy Beers—I really tried to not let that affect me, because it was so intimidating. I did the same scene five or six different ways. Julie Anne said, "We won't do this on set, but let's just try it five different ways with five different intentions behind it." It was the scene with Colin and Penelope at the Rutledge ball, where they're gossiping, and he says to her, "Oh, Penelope, what a barb!" When it was time to do that scene for the real thing, it was a surreal moment.

LUKE NEWTON ON COLIN BRIDGERTON:
Colin is really stuck in the middle. As much as he feels close to Anthony and Benedict, he's always felt he's treated like a kid. He doesn't really like that and doesn't feel like he should be. In Season 1, we see Daphne really blossom into a strong, independent woman, and she's treated with more respect by the family than Colin. I think he's drawn to the idea of not being like every other Bridgerton, of distinguishing himself and not doing exactly what's expected of him. I think that's one of the appeals of Marina, the naughtiness of the affair and his desire to be a man.

This weighs on him: He wants to have a purpose and feel like he can make decisions, like telling Marina that they'll run away to Gretna Green and get married. I think the *idea* of that was a lot more romantic and attractive to him than how he actually felt. In Season 2, you see him struggling with unsettled guilt, which seems to have stolen the enjoyment of his travels and adventures. He may like gossiping in the corner with Penelope, but he didn't want to hurt or negatively affect someone's life. He's probably taking too much responsibility, though, simply because he wants to be a man.

Colin's traveling is the theme of two seasons—it's this constant prompt to suggest he's going to have some excitement in life, something that will make him seem interesting. But I think once he checks it off his list, he feels his lack of purpose and drive even more acutely. It's this "What's next? What do I do next?" feeling, which makes him talk about his travels to anyone who will listen. Particularly Eloise, because she hasn't experienced anything like it, so he can say what he wants and fabricate his journeys and adventures. When you see him with Sir Phillip, and he gets into plants and all these boring specifics, I don't think he is bragging, I think he just finally feels validated. They really have an intimate moment geeking out together.

"The days we don't wear jackets are a real dream, because when we're shooting in the studio it gets quite hot. Anthony always gets to have his sleeves rolled up, and Benedict is the artsy one, so he gets to have different neckties and be a little quirky. But Colin is really just always done up. My character really isn't much of a rebel. So it's a nice moment when Colin is more relaxed, like the bachelor drinks before the wedding."

—Luke Newton

"In the off-season, Penelope and Colin have developed a pen pal relationship, which is very sweet. That said, I think her expectations are a little too high when he comes back because she's been getting his letters and wondering: 'What does this mean?' He really friend zones her. It's just a dagger to her heart."

—Nicola Coughlan

LUKE NEWTON ON COLIN AND PENELOPE:

I think the thing with Colin is that his head is often in the clouds, and he's mistaken by his ambitions and passions. He doesn't have the clarity that his other siblings do. Eloise wants to change the system, Benedict wants to be an artist, Anthony is fulfilling the weight of his familial responsibility, and Colin is just lost, thinking, "Am I in love? Do I want to pursue a career? Am I passionate about anything? Do I want to go on holiday?" He's all over the place but in quite a relaxed way. And then you have Penelope, who is the complete opposite: She's running this secret organization that nobody knows about while keeping her friendships and relationships intact and still supporting the people around her, particularly Colin.

Season 2 starts by establishing something that we don't see but understand: Penelope and Colin have been pen pals for the past year, and as he tells her at the horseback races, "You read and replied to more of my letters than anyone else." So there's a hint that they've gotten to know each other on a different level. Obviously, they grew up together, but there is something more intimate and almost romantic about writing to each other from across the world. But while I think their relationship blossomed, Colin is still unaware of how he may feel.

"Normally, you might get all the scripts at once and really understand the entire arc of your character and the season. But on Season 2, the scripts came in as we were shooting, so we didn't necessarily know how the show was going to end. This actually made it more exciting. I'm guessing it will make it more interesting for viewers to watch as well, because it makes the whole season less predictable. It's hard, as an actor, to suppress the knowledge of what happens to your character and not play to that a little bit throughout. But we really were in the dark!"

—Luke Newton

ELOISE

"I have never understood the fashion for feathers in the hair.
Why would a woman want to draw more notice to the fact that she is
like a bird squawking for a man's attention in some bizarre ritual?"

SHONDA: Eloise is the only true feminist in *Bridgerton*, the one who rails against society with force—and she does it all the time and vocally. While Penelope participates in some of those conversations, Eloise is the one who rejects all of it in the hope for something different for herself. Penelope fervently (and secretly) wants to be in Daphne's shoes; meanwhile, Eloise wants to toss those shoes out the window. Eloise's desperate desire to be more in life than society has deemed appropriate is the show's statement about what happens to women who don't get married.

BETSY: Eloise is so relatable because she feels very modern, but it's important to remember that in the context of the era, she would have been quite radical. And certainly privileged in being able to hate on

society at all because, to quote Penelope, Eloise *is* a Bridgerton. Her family's status grants her a lot of latitude. Plus, Daphne intends to fulfill her role as the oldest—to be the diamond of the season, to marry well, to set up her sisters' future successes. Eloise can dream and explore these other options because Daphne is doing the heavy lifting.

SHONDA: Yes, there's pressure, though Violet is a different kind of mother, bound more by love for her children than an impulse to push them in a certain direction. You can sense her deep affection for them and her desire for them to find happiness. She is tolerant of Eloise's need to resist and willing to give her both space and time, though she does want her to try first, before she rejects society wholesale.

BETSY: I think Violet also recognizes that Eloise doesn't have that much control—she is filterless and guileless in that way, it's one of her most lovable qualities. You can read her face and body before she even opens her mouth.

SHONDA: The others come to her as a sort of truth touchstone, where they can discuss the realities of their lives without varnish or pretense. We certainly see this with Penelope and Daphne, and Eloise's relationship with Benedict is quite beautiful, too, as they both contemplate the ways in which being second in line gives them a certain amount of freedom to resist what is expected of them—though Benedict clearly has far more freedom than she does, and she urges him not to waste it.

BETSY: "Do it, be bold." I love that conversation when she and Benedict share a cigarette and she chastises him for tossing his sketches instead of practicing his drawing. "If you desire the sun and the moon, all you have to do is go out and shoot at the sky—some of us cannot."

DR. HANNAH GREIG: Eloise is a character I particularly love. And not simply because she's funny and feisty. By pushing against the future that she sees laid out for her, and resisting society's expectations, she feels very familiar—and some might say modern. For me, though, she is not simply "modern," but she also captures what some women of the time felt, and we see that in the letters and diaries that remain.

Many daughters of aristocrats, like Eloise, were highly literate. They had access to extensive libraries, they read newspapers, they met interesting people. They were able to engage with new ideas—like what we would now call "women's rights." In Regency England, there were many writers arguing for women's access to education, to politics, to a life beyond marriage and motherhood. There were also those arguing for women's rights to own property and earn their own income, without being dependent on men. This period is often regarded as a time when the first feminist texts became bestsellers, books like Mary Wollstonecraft's *A Vindication of the Rights of Woman*, which forwarded strong, radical arguments for women's equality. Eloise is a character who represents those voices, a chorus that was growing in strength.

CLAUDIA JESSIE: I love Eloise, I relate to her fiercely. She sees the world so clearly and in a way that's so modern. She sees things as they are and imagines the possibilities of what they could be. When Eloise and Penelope are chatting and they're talking about what they want, what they *could* want, and you see them getting excited about *life* and not balls. They are young girls talking about autonomy.

Even though she's so desperate to break out of constraints, there's a real joy to Eloise—she's a live, sparky wire. And as much as she pushes against Daphne's conformity, she also embraces it, in her own way. She's so grateful to her, and they love each other and protect each other. That line at the end is so beautiful and brilliant—a dream line for anyone, really: "Thank you for being so perfect, so that I do not have to be." For Eloise, the idea of being perfect in the eyes of society, of being flawless like a diamond, is the very jail she wants to escape.

She doesn't want to disappoint her family, particularly her mom, but she also really just wants to be free and to take time and unsubscribe from everything she sees around her. She's not anti-love, she just wants to discover slowly but surely what she wants.

What I love about the end of Season 2 is that Eloise doesn't have the revelation that maybe she *does* want to get married—she doesn't really change. But I do love that she expands her mind and gets to

"People always say: 'Eloise is this amazing feminist narrative through the piece.' And I agree, I obviously agree. But I think the show is full of these types of themes: All the boys are struggling with their roles in the family, with their titles and responsibilities, and they all resist the structure of society. I think it shows that the patriarchy really isn't working for anyone, and it's damaging everyone in some way, even those at the very top of it."

—Claudia Jessie

have a crush and feel feelings. It's a credit to the writers that they didn't make Eloise turn coy and internal. Eloise continues to not have any issue expressing all of her emotions. She always says how she feels. It's beautiful that developing a crush does not make her turn inwards. I love how her response is directness: "Hey, I think about you a lot. Do you maybe think about me? And if you can just let me know, that'd be great." It's a clinical, pragmatic, and very Eloise way of going about it. The core of her doesn't change.

Eloise wants to be thought of as a great feminist thinker, sure, but she really just wants the freedom of choice. She wants to meet someone her own way if she is to meet someone at all. First and foremost, Violet wants her children to find love, the love that she had with their father.

She doesn't want to force Eloise into anything, but she also doesn't want Eloise to reject something she's never experienced. I think there is a belief in Violet's heart, that, "Maybe Eloise, if you just tried these things, you would enjoy them. And maybe you will discover that you want to get married." I think that's fair.

Eloise proves that she can meet someone under different circumstances, that she doesn't need to go to tea parties, balls, and carry someone's name on a piece of paper around her wrist. She proves that through her own desire, her own quest, and by following her own interests, she can meet someone. It's great ammo for her: She knows she's capable of developing feelings for someone, on her own terms.

DIRECTOR TRICIA BROCK ON THE DAFFODIL SCENE:

That was a beautiful scene, just beautiful. There aren't enough accolades for Will Hughes-Jones. Chris Van Dusen had seen a field of daffodils when he was scouting in March, but by the time we shot, there were no more daffodils. But Will Hughes-Jones found enough to re-create the moment—real ones for the immediate vicinity, and then the distant ones were artificial. He created a daffodil field that looked absolutely incredible.

Betsy and Shonda
on Enduring Female Friendships

SHONDA: It's interesting that we frequently get questions about enviable friendships like those Penelope and Eloise or Lady Danbury and Queen Charlotte share—it's something that Shondaland shows are known for, apparently. And I never have an appropriate answer, because we don't consider wonderful female friendships to be a style, or a trope, or a ruse. For us, it's reality, and these friendships are born from our own experiences in the world, from characters who are based on real multidimensional women, whether they live in present day or Regency England.

BETSY: Oh, totally. I remember having a conversation with you years ago, when we realized that we rarely see on-screen depictions of realistic friendships. Real friendships are tricky. Real friendships are hard. Real friendships are wonderful and terrific. Enduring friendships go through hills and valleys, it's not a simple road. That's what we're really interested in—not camaraderie between women, per se, but the qualities of a friendship that last. What makes a bond continue versus what makes it break? You see it in Penelope and Eloise—they have several very painful fights and then they find their way back to each other. This is natural.

SHONDA: Everything you're saying could describe our relationship—we've worked as producing partners for a long time. It's the hills and valleys that you mention, the fact that we fight it out. All of these things make it possible for us to work together so successfully. There's a lot of work involved in forming good partnerships—it requires effort, growth, and evolution.

BETSY: I totally agree with that. You know, we're both perfectionists, and we're fundamentally competitive people, and I think that even in the hard times, what's kept us going is the idea that our work always represents the best parts of us. You can be two women who work together for a long time, who are successful, who can serve in different roles and support each other and succeed.

SHONDA: We used to joke that only one of us was allowed to go crazy at a time, but we're often both crazy at the same time. We often both want to quit at the same time. And then we get on the phone, or we get together, and we talk it out, which is such a wonderful privilege. I have someone who is willing to talk through the minutiae of every single part of *Bridgerton*, of every show in our world, and really drill into what is working and what is not.

BETSY: We have to listen. When you and I start to feel off or grumpy, we know it's time to spend time together and reconnect before we get off course. We know we can disagree and recover—we've certainly been there before—but we try to take care of our friendship and partnership so there aren't too many valleys.

ELOISE'S SUMMER READING LIST

MARY WOLLSTONECRAFT
(1759–1797)

Considered one of the founders of feminism, Wollstonecraft focused most of her writing on women's rights. She's most famous for *A Vindication for the Rights of Woman*, in which she argued for equal access to education. She died at the age of thirty-eight, after giving birth to Mary Shelley, the author of *Frankenstein*.

PHILLIS WHEATLEY
(1753–1784)

A former slave, Wheatley was the first African American to publish a book of poetry; she became one of the most famous poets of the nineteenth century.

"In every human Breast, God has implanted a Principle, which we call Love of Freedom; it is impatient of Oppression, and pants for Deliverance."

—Phillis Wheatley

"We never get to do happy endings at Shondaland, so let us have our glory! Let Simon live happily ever after!"
—Shonda Rhimes

THE DUKE OF HASTINGS

"I cannot stop thinking of you. From the mornings you ease to the evenings you quiet to the dreams you inhabit—my thoughts of you never end. I am yours, Daphne. I have always been yours."

SHONDA ON SIMON AND THE IMPORTANCE OF LEADING MEN:
Finding the right leading man is the most important thing you can do. You want somebody who has layers, who can pull off complexity, who is a real actor. You don't want someone who is merely attractive; you need someone who has depth, commitment to character, and can bring something special to the camera.

It was very hard to find the exact right person to play the duke. Regé had been in one of our shows, and he's really good, but I didn't know him personally. I didn't even know he was British. He came in and showed us how he understood Simon in a really brilliant way. Regé is a very serious person—he's really funny, too, but he's very serious when he talks about things that matter. And I liked that about him, as I knew that he would need to approach this character in a way that would give him all the layers needed.

BETSY: Each season of the show is about these characters confronting the obstacle—which they may be conscious or unconscious of—that is keeping them from sharing their heart. In Anthony's case, it's buried. In Simon's case, it's very raw. Simon made a blood pledge to himself and his father that he would never have a child because of the hideous and cruel damage that was inflicted on him as a kid.

SHONDA: He really didn't have a father—or he had a despicable father. Thankfully, he had Lady Danbury, who was a strong and wonderful presence in his life, and likely the reason he turned out as well as he did,

but it doesn't replace the fact that his father was wretched.

BETSY: No, and so you get a man who, in a world where society demands you get married, needs to be a renegade, because he has no intention of fulfilling his duties as a husband. He really feels he cannot. So he develops a lot of coping mechanisms. He travels a lot.

SHONDA: I love the way that's reflected in his wardrobe, the interesting and unusual fabrics, his dressing gown, the jewelry, the furniture that he brings with him, all the bits of flair that feel exotic and not exactly Regency. It really gives him that international flavor, that he's picking up little bits here and there with no real intention to settle down. I thought that was a brilliant way to carry that storyline, that he's not someone who will be pinned down by ambitious mamas.

BETSY: I loved watching the realization dawn on him that he actually does love somebody, that this is what it feels like—and it was so interesting how that idea, for him, is torture. He's found a family in Regency England that everybody looks up to, where all the siblings have a really good time together, where they may fight or converse, but it's incredibly bonded and tight-knit. He's picked the worst possible person to fall in love with. Obviously, she's the best, but in his not rational mind, this is a catastrophe.

SHONDA: A complete catastrophe. He sees no way out—irrational, but then he's built a prison in his own mind.

BETSY: None of our fears are particularly rational. And his vindictiveness toward his father doesn't make sense, either, because the guy is dead; he's only hurting himself. But we all know that feeling, and how hard it is to see the reality of a situation like that. Simon's journey requires that he put that aside and make the leap for something larger, which is love. He has to decide to stop living with the pain of the past, otherwise he would not have a future. He was running in place for years before he met Daphne.

SHONDA: And despite all of his best efforts, she brings him to the truth of who he is and the fact that their love is inescapable.

BETSY: I know the fans think they wanted Simon to return for Anthony's season, but it was never a question, as it would have changed the story. Daphne and Simon got their happy ending. If he were in Season 2, he would have been spending all this time standing in the back, pointing at people, and thinking, "Wow, they're really going through it." I don't think that would have made fans very happy.

SHONDA: No, certainly not, and it wasn't the point, which was to do stand-alone seasons that are essentially complete.

ADJOA ANDOH: On some level, Lady Danbury is saying to Simon, "We all know the truth of how the world is, and you can choose not to join it and participate—but the thing that will make your heart sing is to be loved."

She is effectively telling him that he cannot live in anger and thrive. He doesn't have to get all dumb and booby about it, he can be as clear-eyed as he chooses, but for his soul's sake, love is what he needs to send to himself, and love is what he needs to accept from the world. It is not a soppy thing, it is a hugely demanding thing—harder, in fact, than what he wants to do, which is to turn and go and refuse to be vulnerable. But in that moment, she tells him that he is strong enough to love. Because love is sometimes hard. I love that scene. Like her, he is rich and he has status, and that gives him a lot of power in this world—he can afford to love.

Anatomy of a Scene
THE DUEL

DIRECTOR: SHEREE FOLKSON • EPISODE 104—"AN AFFAIR OF HONOR"

"Simon has decided that he isn't going to hurt Anthony. This isn't about any kind of vengeance or preserving his own life; it's about preserving his own code, the honor of Simon, Daphne, and even Anthony himself. Simon sees himself as a lover and not a fighter—except, of course, the irony is that he is a fighter. Ultimately, it's what guys have done since the beginning of time: get on horses with guns. It's just thick."

—Regé-Jean Page

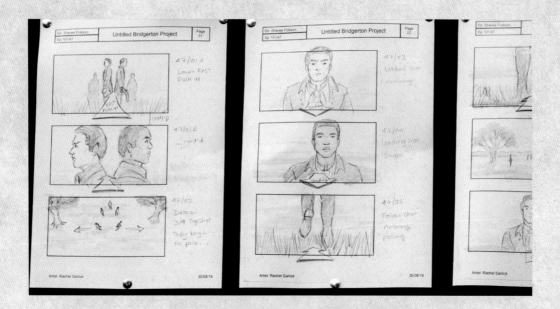

SHONDA: I'm glad that we've evolved, at least, to have better mechanisms for solving our differences than meeting at dawn to shoot each other dead. It's wild that this was perceived as a highly civilized way to problem-solve.

BETSY: What's wilder still is that it was illegal: You would think that these men would rely on the establishment of a boundary to bow out of committing premeditated murder. They had every excuse to find another way.

SHONDA: I like how we employed it in the show, though, because through their desire to heighten the stakes, it gives you a little bit of insight into the characters of these two men. You get the sense that Anthony isn't fixated on Daphne's honor as much as he is on a door to freedom that's slightly cracked open. If he is found out and forced to flee, he recognizes that he might be able to sidestep right out of his responsibility and take off with Siena.

BETSY: I love that moment when Benedict comes home after just having a night of debauchery in the artists' den—and tasting complete freedom—and stumbles into the awareness that if his brother takes off or dies, the fun he was just beginning to enjoy is all done. His face in that moment is priceless.

SHONDA: Meanwhile, Simon thinks he's being honorable: He has such a vendetta against his dead father, and so much pride in upholding a useless pledge he made to spite him, that he would rather be killed by his best friend than marry someone he loves. The logic is insane, and yet it makes perfect sense to him as the moral and right thing to do.

SHEREE FOLKSON: I've done period drama before, and so I have directed duels. It was still challenging, though, because you have all these story beats to get through, and you always want it to feel cinematic when you're watching it on TV. We did some drone shots as well as a top shot of the guys walking away from each other. I also wanted to do a shot where you felt like you were with them. The camera turns with them on steady cam. That was a very specific shot to up the drama and the stakes, and it was very challenging.

DR. HANNAH GREIG ON THE HISTORICAL PRECEDENT OF DUELING:

Duels have a very long history as a system of resolving manly honor among aristocracy. They were used for settling all sorts of arguments or differences of opinion. They might have been about politics, social insults, or issues of marriage and matters of the heart. Duels were illegal, so they were typically fought in public, at dawn, when nobody else was around. It seems insane now, but gentlemen of Simon's rank would routinely turn to the duel as their primary way of solving disputes. At their inception, the men used swords; by Regency times, pistols were the weapon of choice. And while sometimes people would shoot guns into the air, duels were often deadly!

"The duel scene was a brilliant way to capture how high the stakes were for these men, and also how they impose their will on women. Really, it was just a game of chicken, and the male ego was such that they would continue until someone would fall away. Fortunately, at least in this instance, that doesn't happen—it could have, simply because they're both so very stubborn."

—Jonathan Bailey

FRANKI HACKETT—DAPHNE'S STUNT DOUBLE—ON PULLING OFF THE FALL: Daphne's appearance is critical to bring this scene to a peaceful conclusion, but I had to fall off a horse to achieve it. I wear loads of padding with built-in shock absorption all over my body, though you can certainly land funny, and you will always get bruised. For this stunt, my job is to race in, then the horse rears, and I fall off onto my mark. Fortunately, I did it in one take!

JESS BROWNELL ON HOW THE DUEL MIGHT HAVE GONE:

We wanted to really express the prison of womanhood that these women were up against. We wanted the guns out and to be sure that there were actual stakes to that encounter. One pitch in the room by Jonathan Igla was that either Anthony or Simon accidentally shoot the horse that Daphne rides in on.

And so we were like, "Yes! Yes, that's it, everyone will fall, and the viewer will wonder if Daphne is dead. No, the horse is dead." But then we got to the next step: What are they going to do with the dead horse?

It was a long conversation before we reminded ourselves that we are writing a romance show, and does anyone really want to see an animal get shot? Probably not. So for us, it was about constantly finding that line between what feels high stakes without taking it to too dark of a place.

The
FEATHERINGTON
FAMILY

PENELOPE

"Do not pity me, either."

SHONDA: Penelope is delightful to me; there is something very special about her and the way she is always hoping for something—I like her very, very much.

BETSY: Yes, she longs and hopes for Colin, definitely—she is nursing a serious crush. But in some ways, he's just an object for the acceptance and security that she craves, a safe harbor from her rejecting family. He's a lovely guy and cute, but he may not be a match for her intelligence.

SHONDA: She is inarguably brilliant—and she can certainly write! It's interesting to me that while Penelope is the keenest observer of society in the show, she still feels like someone who is trapped in a world she doesn't quite understand. Or perhaps it's just that her wide-eyed romantic optimism keeps crashing into the reality of what's actually available to her. She is someone whose face is pressed up against the glass of other people's lives.

BETSY: And that hurts, to notice the world while it pays no attention to you. While Penelope is so kind—you really get a sense of her empathy because she has lived so much of her life as an outsider—it's interesting how she deflects and diffuses her pain in a constructive way. Even though Lady Whistledown is biting and causes damage, and perhaps it's not "nice" to write a scandal sheet, there is something very revolutionary and likely healing about censuring a society that deserves the criticism. There are so many things about which Penelope is very naive—sex, most tellingly—and yet she understands exactly how to land her words, like a rock in a still pond.

SHONDA: As an observer, she very much understands the difference between what it means to be a Bridgerton and what it means to be a Featherington—her awareness of social status far exceeds that of Eloise, in part because she is constrained by being the latter. To be a Bridgerton is to be gilded, and there's no question that they will each marry well. Meanwhile, Penelope is like, "Look at who we are, look how I'm dressed, look at how my mother is a social climber." That rage moment with Eloise in Season 1—"You are a Bridgerton, you don't have to worry about anything"—is so poignant because it's true. It's one thing to rail against a society that embraces you; it's another thing entirely to want to be part of a world that sees you as an outsider.

BETSY: Yes, her frustration and despair are palpable and very human. So many of us know what it feels like to be on the outskirts, desperate to join and yet also wanting to reject—and, in her case, punish—a society that would reject her first. And it gives her an incredible amount of power: As she remarks at one point, even Queen Charlotte lacks a pen.

NICOLA COUGHLAN: I love the yin and yang of Penelope—between her insides and her outsides, between her and Eloise, between her and Lady Whistledown. She's quite complicated and polarized: She processes her understanding of her world through Lady Whistledown but not her emotions. I played two roles with Penelope and always needed to be aware that there was what was happening in her life, that everyone could see, and also what was happening around her in the moment, that Lady Whistledown was observing and writing. When people rewatch the show after knowing my second identity, they will start to see how I managed to always be there in the vicinity. Because Penelope is so invisible and overlooked, I disappeared into the background. But at key moments, like when Daphne bumps into Simon for the first time, or when she walks down the stairs and drops her fan in front of the prince, or when Simon leaves as she's dancing with the prince, I'm front row to the interaction. I'm always watching, even if nobody is watching me.

She was such an interesting character to play. She's so shy and low status, and yet she's also the most powerful woman in London. She has very little life experience, and she's not particularly streetwise, but she's very, very intelligent. And she thinks she knows a lot more about life than she actually does. There's a certain cockiness to her [in Season 2], which makes sense: If you walked around and everyone was saying how great you were all the time and constantly obsessing about your true identity, that would of course have an effect on you.

FEATHERINGTON FAMILY DYNAMICS

HARRIET CAINS: Shoveling us all out on the marriage mart at the same time was apparently a classless thing to do at the time. That's why our presentation to the queen was ridiculous, the three of us trying to squeeze ourselves through that door. I think of Polly Walker as Kris Jenner and obviously, I'm her favorite daughter. I don't know if that's me just *hoping* I'm the favorite daughter, but Philippa thinks of herself as a mini of her mom.

BESSIE CARTER: These girls have no real agency, despite the fact that they're in the loudest dresses and have the most vibrant hair in the room. It's still not enough to attract attention. They are just waiting for someone to say yes to them, and that's quite frustrating. We just keep missing the mark, failing to catch anyone's eye.

HARRIET: Ultimately, there's tons of dysfunction, but we can fuck with each other because no one else will. There is love and solidarity to the family, along with a fair amount of savageness. I think it's the dad's fault, to be honest—Lady Featherington picks up a lot of the slack that he didn't provide.

BESSIE: They're in direct competition even though they're very close. They really need each other. And yes, they bicker, as all sisters do—but you need that silliness and irritant as a foil for the heartfelt moments that they have. And they have those in spades. There's not really any love in that house except between the sisters. If you look carefully, they're always together—even when Penelope is present—and they sit close. When they find out Lord Featherington is dead, they hold hands.

BESSIE: I love playing the characters who people find annoying but secretly want to succeed. I very much felt this way about poor Prudence. Oh, Prudence. She's the oldest—the closest to her mother—but she's also teetering toward spinsterhood. And her entire life has been engineered for finding a match, so this is actually a really terrible fate. She has nothing else in her life. That is the only thing that she's been brought up to want and to do—her mother doesn't want them to read, to fill their heads with thoughts, she just wants them to find a man, any man.

You imagine those girls at the ball every night, all night long. They never get asked to dance. They're bored, sad, rejected. It's really a terrible fate! That's one of the reasons I turned Prudence into a drinker—if she's going to stand on her feet all night, she may as well chug champagne. It's very relatable!

HARRIET: I like to think that I'm very smart, or not as dumb as Philippa. But that was the brief, though I got to add a few dimensions. In the first season, she is very naive and desperate, and there really wasn't much of a difference between her and Prudence status-wise. But in the second season, as a married woman, I really got to play a progression. *Mean Girls* was a big influence, actually—Season 2, Philippa is not much smarter, but she's definitely more of a Regina George with some status among the plastics.

MARINA

"Well, should I perhaps entrap a bad man, then?"

SHONDA: Marina is an outsider in so many ways: She's from the country, she's from a different class, she's Black in this white family, and most impossibly, she believes in love. Even in the process of realizing that she's pregnant, she maintains hope that her love, George, will come for her. It's terrible to watch the show evolve and time pass: the not knowing, the feeling a fool, the general despair about her future, the recognition that she is truly a prisoner to her fate. And all the while, you can sense that she knows she's felt love and she will not give that up easily for a match in the marriage mart.

BETSY: It's unclear what's most painful: the doubt she begins to hold about George's feelings and intentions—was he a villain?—or the recognition that she must start playing the game and strategize for a solution before time runs out. She's also all alone.

SHONDA: I had a tremendous amount of sympathy for Marina, particularly because she unwittingly makes Penelope her rival, and there's a lot of love in the world for Penelope. I don't want to trivialize Penelope's infatuation for Colin, but from where Marina stands after George has seemingly abandoned her, love is, at best, fleeting and, at most, a lie. In the same way Lady Featherington feels like she's doing Marina a ser-

vice by underlining the reality of her situation within society, in some ways, Marina is just paying it forward for Penelope and telling her that an unrequited crush is just that.

BETSY: Meanwhile, she starts to take control of her future: She strategizes at the Modiste, and she snaps to in order to take advantage of Colin's crush on her. It's her best path for saving herself and her baby, for "a glimpse of happiness," as she explains. Fans are really hard on her, but men made strategic moves all the time—for an heir, for status—without condemnation. She is effectively doing the same, just looking for safe passage. It's impossible to blame her when the other two options are being cast out of society and left to squalor or shacking up with a gouty old bachelor. There is no ideal outcome.

KELLY VALENTINE HENDRY: We called Ruby Barker back for a second audition because we needed to know if she could tear down Lady Whistledown. And she was incredible. Not only did she pull off the scene, but she walked into the casting room and knew every person's name and exactly what they did and who they were. She shook everyone's hand. She approached it like a business meeting. It was incredibly impressive.

The
SHARMA FAMILY

BETSY: In the middle of Season 1, we started talking about Kate's family, and we decided we wanted to represent a different part of the world of color. Historically, there is a deep and entrenched connection between India and England, and we loved the idea of including this beautiful Indian family—of the manor born—incorporated into society. It's such an organic part of British history. The obstacle that they face comes from the fact that the mother didn't marry as her family wanted: She married a merchant. The obstacle had nothing to do with anything but class, which I thought was just great, and another way to play with things.

SHONDALAND EXEC ANNIE LAKS: Simone had made a comment to our casting director, Kelly Valentine Hendry, that we should look at Charithra for Edwina because they both have Tamil heritage, which refers to a specific region in Southeast Asia, not knowing that we were already trying to make that happen. We then did a chemistry read between Simone, Jonny, and Charithra on Zoom, and I actually had tears in my eyes because it was so perfect.

"Truly being in the inner circle meant that you had connections in the right networks, you were invited to the right balls, you had patronage from the right hostesses, and that the powerful matriarchs like Lady Danbury knew who you were and vouched for you." —Dr. Hannah Greig

KATE

"I take issue with any man who views women merely as chattels and breeding stock."

BETSY: Kate is very interesting. Like Anthony, she's suffered a fair amount of trauma in her life. And similar to Anthony, she believes that her role in her family is solely to take care of Edwina and ensure she gets what she needs. What Kate wants and is interested in has never been a question. She's never allowed herself to imagine what that could be; she's never allowed herself to indulge in that.

SHONDA: As Season 2 evolves, it's clear that she has no idea that she even has wants and desires, because she's simply assumed it's not her place to.

BETSY: She's almost like a stage mom. Every single thing she might have hoped or wished or dreamed of for herself, she has put on Edwina. And Edwina calls her out on that. And I get it. Her mother died, then her father died, and her stepmother is more like a friend than a parent—Mary is lovely, but she's frail and not really a problem solver. Kate took it upon herself to become the mother and leader of the family. And for both financial as well as emotional rea-

sons, she wants to make sure that Edwina is taken care of—though it's important to Kate that it's with someone who will love her and make her happy.

SHONDA: Yes, she's a few steps ahead of Anthony on that learning curve—she's not trying to dispense with Edwina, or even find the most advantageous match, she just wants her to be with a good person. When do you think Kate realizes she likes Anthony?

BETSY: I think it's that moment in the croquet match where she finally drops her guard and gets playful and throws the ball next to the gravestone. Simone Ashley does this amazing thing as an actress where she can just drop the hardness from her face, and we see that in the moment. It's arguable when it turns to attraction, but that's the first moment where you see a hint of playful vulnerability.

SHONDA: Yes, I love it when she screws up her face. It's funny that as someone who is so obsessed with controlling herself—and

the lives of everyone else around her—she is also the easiest to read.

BETSY: Yep, that's Kate's other major arc: She has to submit to her own emotions. She's a control freak. Kate is very used to everyone doing what she says. She calls the shots. And she gets to Mayfair, and that's just not happening: Lady Danbury doesn't do what she says, Anthony doesn't do what she says, the dog isn't really doing what she says. She's not used to not being in charge. Their love affair is very much a war of the wills. They really do vex each other.

SHONDA: And yet they can't stay away.

ANNIE LAKS: We had a very specific vision for Kate. Simone Ashley was always in consideration, but she was cast in a movie, and so we didn't know if the timing would work. But we had her and Jonny do a chemistry reading in person, which was so helpful—and then it was hard to see Kate as anyone but Simone.

SIMONE ASHLEY: I auditioned just as the show was coming up, and Phoebe and Regé's faces were everywhere—the audition process was very fast. I received a text that casting was interested in seeing me, and within fourteen days I went from self-taping and Zoom auditions to meeting Jonny Bailey and having a chemistry read with him. Before I knew it, I was receiving scripts and taking creative meetings and doing wig fittings and horseback training and dance lessons.

SIMONE ASHLEY ON PLAYING KATE: I love Kate, I think she's an incredible character. She's a bit of an outsider, and a bit of a loner, and definitely *not* a people pleaser. She isn't afraid to be opinionated or controversial, which is what makes the love story so amazing. Anthony and Kate are quite similar, and the story requires patience: I think that's the strongest love you can give someone, that patience. Anthony has a rare patience for her because she has a very tough exterior, and she's feisty and strong-willed and hardheaded, and he can relate to her deeply. Like Anthony, she is protecting a soft vulnerability and heart, and she's incredibly complicated. She had a hard path, history, and life raising Edwina.

I admire Kate's values, her priorities within her family, and her authenticity. She isn't afraid to do what she feels honestly in the moment, but she has to learn to let her guard down and grow and change. She has to learn that you don't always have to do things alone and independently and that there's strength in seeking help and having someone to love and take care of you.

At the beginning, Kate really wants to fade into the background: She isn't there to find love and a husband. She wants to marry Edwina off, take care of her family, and then run away back to India to be on her own. She doesn't wear makeup, she doesn't have her bust out like the other ladies of the ton.

But the more she loosens her heart and frees herself, you see that with her hair. The makeup starts to pop as well as she begins to explore her femininity. The colors become more bright and beautiful and more blue,

which I think is a nod to the fact that she is really destined to be a Bridgerton.

Anthony and Kate are very similar: They both hold a lot of responsibility and duty, and they're deeply misunderstood. They have very complicated paths and a lot of trauma, particularly associated with their fathers. I would imagine they've gone through their lives without meeting anyone who really understands them. When they meet each other, there's obvious chemistry, but there's also a fire that they initially associate with hatred. But with more time and space, they allow whatever is between them to evolve and grow, which translates itself into love and understanding. It's a very special and challenging love story.

Anthony is so used to being the playboy of the Regency era, of getting all the girls and having ladies fall at his feet. Kate is unfamiliar: She's isn't afraid to say what she thinks of him or to challenge him. She stops him in his tracks. He also challenges her because he doesn't give up and has patience for her. She's really not used to that, or holding that sort of attention.

THE HALADI SCENE

CHARITHRA CHANDRAN: I love the *haladi* scene that I do with my mother and sister before the wedding, because it was such an honor to introduce something that is so known and important in my culture.

SIMONE ASHLEY: We shot the *haladi* scene with Tom Verica, and I explained how my mom used to mix flour to make the paste, and Tom said, "Do that. Do it that way, in a way that's personal to you." Even thinking about that is wild. I never thought I'd be on a set doing that, particularly in a period drama. It's incredible.

EDWINA

*"What I am, Kate, is a grown woman. And for the first time in my life
I am able to make a decision based on what I would like."*

BETSY: In some ways, at the beginning of Season 2, it's like Kate and Edwina are one person: If you split a person in two and Kate took the strategy and Edwina took the fun stuff, you'd get a complete person. Edwina does nothing but try to please Kate. She tries to be exactly who Kate wants her to be. She's willing to let Kate make all her decisions. Edwina's journey is to figure out who the hell she actually is when it occurs to her that everything she's been told is a lie. It requires acknowledging that she deserves to be loved, to have a life that is rich and fulfilling.

SHONDA: That may be true, but Edwina has to grow up to realize that. It's on Edwina to get that for herself. She can't rely on Kate

to make decisions on her behalf. Her character arc is to recognize that and then take responsibility for so easily seceding control and letting herself be babied.

BETSY: Up to the point where Edwina realizes she's been hornswoggled, she's bordering on smug. She comes in hot: "I know every language, I dance perfectly, I can make conversation, I'm perfectly charming, I'm not going to get in your way." She's clearly confident that's the case and not at all surprised when she is anointed as the diamond, even if she doesn't know what that means. When she meets Anthony, she realizes he's the gold ring. That she's the most eligible woman in the pond for this particular season, and he's her equivalent, and he is what she should want. They will be the homecoming king and queen. They will make a beautiful pair.

SHONDA: Oh yes, in her mind, they're the perfect wedding toppers. It's perfect, it's predetermined, it makes sense. And it's a story as old as time—we want what feels just so slightly out of reach. Even though they're betrothed, she can sense that she doesn't quite have him. She just doesn't realize why.

BETSY: But this isn't Kate's first subterfuge. Kate's been keeping secrets from Edwina for years. Edwina deserves to know the situation, and Kate keeps her from it, thinking, of course, that she's protecting her. But really, Kate thinks she is the only one who can handle it. To be fair, Edwina's ignorance doesn't help—she really doesn't ask questions.

CHARITHRA CHANDRAN ON GETTING CAST AS EDWINA:

I knew playing Edwina would be a real challenge because she is so different than how I am in real life—I'm much more of a Kate. It would have been really easy to make her overly sweet and saccharine, but I made a commitment to her to portray her with respect and dignity and really ground her. I didn't want her to seem like an angel, but more like a fully formed human.

SIMONE ASHLEY: Edwina overcomes a lot of wrongs that have been done to her, and that requires a very strong, forgiving person. Edwina may learn a lot from Kate, but she also has a lot to teach her—I think Kate ultimately learns more, which is a really nice twist.

CHARITHRA CHANDRAN: Edwina is such an interesting character because, like any human, she is not wholly good, even though that's the first impression. Edwina's flaw, really, is that she is a bit self-involved. She wants her sister to find someone and is excited about the prospect of Mr. Dorset as a suitor for her, but she doesn't have nearly as much energy for her sister's happiness as her sister does for hers. It would be very easy to think, "Oh, poor Edwina, look at what Kate's done," but it's not that simple. To be fair, Edwina only focuses on herself because everyone only focuses on her.

SIENA

SHONDA: *Bridgerton* is about women—and we meant all women. Including those who weren't considered "ladies," to quote Anthony. That designation actually applied to a very small circle of tightly constrained high-society women—the others, like Siena, were shut out from status, but there were many other upsides for them, including the opportunity to pick their path.

BETSY: Yes, women like Siena had far more theoretical freedom—and yet far less "value." Anthony lusts for her—he may even love her, to the best of his ability at that point in his life—but she is not on the table for him as an option for marriage. It's clear he hasn't even considered it. As she says, she is the woman he loves in the darkness, and it never seems to occur to him to contemplate what that must feel like for her.

SHONDA: Siena represents for me the very dark underbelly to this society—she's a gifted opera singer, and a stunning and smart girl, and yet she must find a man to support her. Someone who will be her champion and take care of her. Unlike Madame Delacroix, who runs her own business, Siena needs a patron—and that typically comes in the form of a type of prostitution. She clearly has strong feelings for Anthony, but not at the expense of her own survival. She remains very clear-eyed about the realities and practicalities of her situation, and the specific power she has to wield, which is her beauty and talent and sexual prowess. She recognizes that she needs to capitalize on this appeal to ensure her needs are met. She has that great line, "I am no innocent debutante. Gentlemen certainly do not engage me for that."

SABRINA BARTLETT: I think Siena has one of the most interesting character arcs: She chooses herself. The juiciest part is the push and pull between her and Anthony, and the palpable fear that they both feel—one stepping out and offering, the other betraying. They are scared and are metaphorically leaving each other out to dry, abandoned. That final scene, when she tells Anthony to let her go . . . I still get goose bumps thinking about it. So many women can relate to that moment, when you're pushed to the edge and you recognize that you are strong enough to say, "No, no more. I choose myself, I choose me."

JULIA QUINN ON SIENA: I loved this character, even though she only gets a glancing mention in *The Viscount Who Loved Me,* where her name is Maria. I love what they did with her, the ways in which they gave her this whole world—it really provides a counterpoint to the rest of the women.

GENEVIEVE DELACROIX

SHONDA: I laughed out loud when I learned from Jess Brownell that Madame Delacroix is named for LaCroix water, a writers' room staple—but it's kind of perfect for her. Because she's a British girl with a cockney accent who is pretending to be French in order to set herself apart within the ton—and to create an air of exoticism.

BETSY: The irony, of course, is that she doesn't need to be exotic—she's already exotic simply by running her own business and doing as she pleases. Unlike the women of the ton, she has freedoms—and unlike Siena, who needs a man of stature to effectively pay her way, she supports herself. She's not constrained by "polite society"; she has a thriving business and likely employs dozens of other women; she is making and spending her own money. She dresses like a man if she likes, she smokes hashish, she has threesomes. I mean, Madame Delacroix is really living!

SHONDA: She is definitely creatively expressed! It's interesting to me that she feels like she needs any artifice at all—though it makes you wonder whether she puts on the accent to make herself feel better, or to simply codify the egos of the women whom she dresses, since Paris was the mecca for high fashion, as it is now. Her accent certainly didn't hurt business!

BETSY: Yeah, I don't think she suffers from low esteem. I think she sees fashion society for exactly what it is—she's amused by it, she loves the hot gossip, but at the end of the day, she can take it or leave it. She's certainly not left breathless by brushing up against these fancy ladies. But she'll happily take their money and spend it how she wants.

KATHRYN DRYSDALE: I was never given Genevieve's backstory, so I was able to be a bit fluid with what I was creating, which is always a nice luxury. I knew Genevieve had a lot of agency and created a persona for survival—she created it for those women who were buying her dresses and spending a lot of money. Apparently, it was quite common at the time to mimic Parisienne dressmakers, because the best tailors were coming from France. So to compete, British modistes pretended they were French.

To do research, I studied a modern-day tailor named Zack Pinsent. He does tutorials on Instagram and is quite famous, with a huge following. He makes Regency clothing for people in a historically accurate way. I watched a lot of his work and researched modistes at the time. Ultimately, I developed two different physicalities: I'm much slouchier and more relaxed in my body when I'm Genevieve and hanging out with Siena and Benedict. My rhythm is very different, and my tone is also quite high. But when I'm working with customers as Madame Delacroix, I hold myself as tall as possible, drop my voice so that it becomes a bit breathy, and slow all of my movements down.

"The way that we typically reconstruct worlds for period pieces is through a lot of research: We look at sketches, paintings, periodicals, papers, and try to best guess or approximate how various effects were achieved and how the worlds were constructed. Sometimes historians know, but often things are too niche. It requires a lot of experimentation and head-scratching to arrive at something that perfectly approximates the past using today's technology."

—Will Hughes-Jones

BUILDING THE WORLD

"*I remember going to the production design office one day to meet the incredible team of artists bringing the world to life, and not only did they have Whistledowns printing on a period-appropriate press, but they had options—different cameos and text types. The number of pieces they designed to round out and create the world were endless. I felt completely transported. They weren't simply sets dressed up like homes—you felt like you were in this world. They contain subtle details that are easy to miss, but the consideration of every single detail makes every scene seem immersive and alive.*"

—Betsy Beers

The Complexities of Production

SHONDALAND HEAD OF PRODUCTION SARA FISCHER:

All of my friends always tell me how sorry they are for me that I have to work the whole time I'm away on a production. And my response is, "Are you kidding me?" I get access to places that you never get to see as a tourist. We get dropped off at the front door of these incredible homes and get to go behind the ropes. I remember the first time I saw the Bridgerton House dressed up in wisteria—it was as if it was a painting.

In hindsight, opting to do our first show with Netflix as a gigantic period drama in a country where we had never worked before was maybe not the smartest decision. It was just a colossal undertaking, with a few scary hairpin turns that made it extra exciting and, to put it lightly . . . logistically challenging! Typically, we need sixteen to eighteen weeks in the UK to get a production really rolling, then once you start, you have to go, go, go: The train is running down the tracks, and it is cost-prohibitive to bring it to a grinding halt. This is particularly true in the UK, where there are a lot of period dramas filming—there are only so many period locations that allow people to film, so you're competing with other productions. And you're also competing with people who are having big parties or getting married at the same sites.

The other hurdle about filming in the United Kingdom when it comes to production is that they are much more sensible about their lives: They don't do overtime like we do here in the States. They know that if they show up at eight a.m., they are going home at six p.m. We needed to plan for additional days in the shooting sched-

ule. We set up shop and started building our sets in a former carpet warehouse—a huge industrial space with forty-foot ceilings. The offices were beautiful, the sets were incredible, and we were ready to roll. And then it rained, as it is likely to do in London, and the roof caved in. We were seven weeks out from the start of filming.

Because we had to start building our sets from scratch—again—we had to redo our entire production calendar and shoot the show in a wild way: We traveled to and shot all of our locations first, from July through December, and then we brought each director back after we rebuilt the sets. It was a traveling shitshow, in the best possible way.

The viewer would never know the complexity that went on behind the scenes, moving hundreds of cast and crew around the entire country and housing them in small villages. Just finding enough hotel rooms was a feat—one of the many small miracles the production team pulled off. Keep in mind that every character, background actor, and dancer went through the hands of ten to fifteen people before they arrived on set, receiving makeup, hair, and costuming from undergarments to outer garments to jewelry. This was on a scale that's almost impossible to imagine.

And it wouldn't be exciting if there weren't plenty of last-minute changes to keep us busy: We're often asked to pivot quickly. For example, the Sharmas were originally going to have their own house on Grosvenor Square for the season, and that's what we planned for in production. After building the sets, we learned they would live with Lady Danbury, and so Will recycled the house into Lady Danbury's house. We changed it all, including the colors, to make it that beautiful soft pink. We always manage to keep it going.

PRODUCER SARADA MCDERMOTT: Sometimes I would wake up and not know what city I was in because we were on the road filming for seventeen weeks. It was a traveling circus. Perhaps one of the biggest challenges in Season 1 were the balls, which was a heavy production lift, to put it lightly. We themed as many as possible simply because we were struggling to make them look different. We needed fire-breathers, we needed performers in cages, we needed drama, volume, and color!

ALISON EAKLE: Frankly, we don't always know what will be hard to do in production or visual effects. Even though balls were how the ton interacted and how young people could flirt while chaperoned, we ended up needing to reduce the number. We knew the audience and the production team would quickly get ball fatigue, so we used promenading in Hyde Park as an opportunity to bring the marriage mart together. That's also why we introduced the boxing match and why Season 2 has a big horse race.

SARADA: It's funny now, but Chris kept promising that he would stop writing balls. (He didn't.)

SARA FISCHER ON DEALING WITH COVID:

Season 1 wrapped just as the pandemic was starting. I think we flew people back to the States two weeks before lockdown. But Season 2 started a year into the pandemic. It was quite a feat to not only get through COVID filming a show of this size but also to be successful at it. It was definitely stressful. Because of the sheer number of people we were working with, we needed a lot of additional space and equipment. Our number one priority was creating the safest environment to bring people back to. As we planned, we realized we had challenges. We couldn't put the same number of people in a makeup trailer, we needed to distance out crowd scenes, and we needed ginormous tents on locations in order to feed everyone and still social-distance.

Production delays are one thing—that's just money and time—but we had a real fear of people getting ill. No producer wanted to call an actor or crew member and tell them that they had been exposed to COVID.

It was a major testament to our Season 2 producer, Michelle Wright. It was her first time doing an episodic show, but she really did an incredible job. Michelle said that each block of filming two episodes of *Bridgerton* was equivalent to producing the movie *Cruella*, which she had just finished. She was blown away by the scale. She produced "four Cruellas" during COVID.

SEASON 2 PRODUCER MICHELLE WRIGHT ON THE COMPLICATIONS OF COVID:

We were in the heart of COVID lockdown when Sara Fischer called me about *Bridgerton* Season 2. As a movie producer, I'm used to big-scale production, but *this was a big show*: We were testing five to six hundred people a day for COVID, and the production ran for about 150 days. At the time, you couldn't have more than two people in a van with windows open, so you can imag-

ine that with 150 supporting artists, you need an incredible amount of transportation. Our security and transportation footprint was *enormous*. Fortunately, we had an incredible production team—there were about eight of us in the main office, includ-

ing secretaries, coordinators, assistants, COVID supervisors, and Simon Fraser, our incredible line producer. Ultimately, it was an incredible community effort and a very human situation—everyone was a team player and was so kind about it.

Bringing the Ton Together

SHONDA: There are so many balls in *Bridgerton*—they're one of the primary mechanisms for bringing the ton together, when we get to see the whole ensemble cast interact in a single space. As you can imagine, the amount of work that goes into each one is staggering. Every ball needs to be fully designed, costumed, choreographed, and set to music before we can even begin to figure out how to film all the interactions between the actors.

BETSY: Because things really happened at those balls. They were the center of social life. Director Julie Anne Robinson said that at Lady Danbury's ball in Season 1, she needed to film more than thirty interactions as Anthony and Daphne moved through the ballroom. To establish that world and those moments from every angle and make it seamless for the viewer is an incredible feat.

SHONDA: It's a good metaphor for how it would have felt to go to a ball like that at the time—you are there to be seen, certainly, and most important for the debutantes, to arrange the partnership that will define the rest of your life, but you were also tracking the movements and interactions of everyone else in the room. Most balls included a guest list of a thousand. Honestly, my feet hurt just thinking about this.

BETSY: And for many of these young women, these balls are the first times they've been out in society, on display. It's like going to prom every night of the week, chaperoned by your parents. A potent cocktail of anxiety, self-consciousness, curiosity, excitement, and desire—all on a very grand, heightened scale.

SHONDA: And in a corset. So no matter how breathless you might feel at the spectacle and the potential for romance, you can't breathe. Panting while chasséing would have been frowned upon, too.

BETSY: I would imagine they'd also be incredibly hot—middle of the summer, no air-conditioning, and hundreds of high-society people sweating their makeup off. It certainly explains why the women loved those fans! Apparently, that's also why they chalked the floors with elaborate designs, so that dancers wouldn't slip on their butts. It sounds unbearable and anxiety-producing, yet at the same time, you can imagine how it would seem so romantic and fun.

Anatomy of a Scene
LADY DANBURY'S BALL

DIRECTOR: JULIE ANNE ROBINSON • EPISODE: 101—"DIAMOND OF THE FIRST WATER"

LOCATION: assembly rooms, Bath

KEY SONG: "Thank U, Next" by Vitamin String Quartet

BEST LINE: "The most perfect thing for you to do now is not to dance. But to leave them all wanting more. If anyone knows how this works, it is your eldest brother."
—ANTHONY BRIDGERTON

KEY OCCURRENCE: Daphne and Simon chest-bump! (and meet)

CAST: Principles, plus 140 supporting artists, including: 6 Danbury footmen, 24 dancers, 4 mamas, 43 high society ladies, 42 high society men, 13 military, and 8 musicians.

CREW: Principles, plus 1 home economist, 2 SFX supervisors, 2 choreographers, 6 camera operators, 4 electricians, 31 customers, 44 hair and makeup artists, 3 medics, 3 sound technicians, dialect coach, etiquette advisor.

JULIE ANNE ROBINSON: This is one of the most interactive scenes in the entire show—the Bridgertons arrive, and everybody is looking at them as they promenade around the room; it's the moment when Anthony is already beginning to turn suitors away. There's a lot of other activity as well: Nigel Berbrooke makes his move, Colin spots Marina and joins the swarm, Simon and Daphne meet, the Featheringtons rush the duke. There are thirty-three different interactions to capture, each with its own specific setup, including a lot of dialogue. In order to capture the sound, all of the dancers had earpieces hidden beneath their wigs—tiny, tiny little speakers—so they could hear the music while they were dancing, but the room was otherwise completely silent outside of the actors, who knew exactly where they had to be because it was choreographed down to the very last step.

"The chandeliers were supposedly worth five million pounds . . . each. I heard they were on a pulley system, so the cinematographer, Jeff Jur, and I decided that we should lower the chandeliers significantly so that they were just above the heads of the dancers, ensuring they'd be in every shot. The scary part is that we had a technocrane operating, which is a huge arm for a camera so you can get those high sweeping shots. There were a few moments where I had to hold my breath because that technocrane came oh so close to those chandeliers."

—Julie Anne Robinson

"Hosting balls was a major status symbol. During the London season—which lasted for six months—every duchess hosted one. They'd all exchange letters from their country homes to ensure that they didn't cross wires and send out invites for the same night, since, for the most part, they were corralling the same crowd. Homes would be especially decorated for the evening, there'd be incredible food, music, and entertainment. In Bridgerton, Lady Danbury hosts the opening ball of the season—you can trust that this is a privilege granted to only the most powerful hostess of the ton."

—Dr. Hannah Greig

"All of the balls had a different number of dancers, depending on the size of the room and how many cast we were working with and the number of musicians who also needed to be accommodated. Julie Anne's ball at Danbury Hall was a magical day and quite huge. She staged her ball like an opera, it was epic. I remember the rehearsal for this ball so clearly—it was the hottest day of the year! We had twenty-four dancers, whereas with Tom's balls, we typically worked with twelve dancers who filmed four balls in eight days. Those were all shot in different rooms of the same building, and they were not of the same physical scale. Tom staged it to bring out details that we hadn't even thought about. But four balls in eight days! Tom Verica is my hero!"

—Jack Murphy

"Members of Regency society spent a vast amount on their wardrobes because every dress was scrutinized: They were always on a stage, even if they were just promenading in Hyde Park. It's probably useful to think of that world as a permanent red carpet— and similar to red carpets today, what was worn by this world drove fashion trends for the rest of the country."

—Dr. Hannah Greig

Costume Design

ELLEN MIROJNICK ON BUILDING A
COSTUME HOUSE FROM THE GROUND UP:

Dressing the entire ton was a massive undertaking. The design formula was to create hundreds of basic garments that we could then embellish and differentiate from each other. We decided on three or four different silhouettes for both the men and the women and then created a process I call "stack and stitch." The cutters stack the fabric and cut thirty dresses at a time. We had makers in Budapest, Madrid, and New York stacking and stitching, including a brilliant tailor named Gabor who did the men's vests, jackets, and pants.

Once the base garments are done, they go to the embellishers, who make sure each piece is different. We always said that the Bridgertons were a French macaroon and the Featheringtons were citrus fruit, and so we used those as spokes of the wheels for the world of costumes.

Assistant costumer John Glaser created a spectacular world of background characters who were full of layers, and he did bespoke fittings on every single supporting artist as if they were principal cast—which is not typical. We pushed the costumers to a creative point they had never been to before, because this version of Regency England was entirely new to them.

We made seventy-five hundred pieces of costume, including all of the period-specific underwear—and that doesn't account for all the shoes and jewelry we made. That's a staggering amount.

ELLEN ON SHONDA'S FIRST VIEWING:
As is typical with Shondaland, ahead of filming, Shonda wanted to have a look-see at the costuming to see how we were getting along. It was an electric moment. We assembled our entire palette and put up all the inspiration pictures. We put these wonderful embroidered nightgowns up on stands, but we also wanted her to see how we were going to adapt the silhouette for *Bridgerton,* and so we put a basic magenta dress on a stand.

The silhouette was correct, but as I was sitting there with the department, looking at it, I knew we hadn't blurred the lines enough. It was a very on-period dress in a beautiful color, and I thought to myself: "No, it can't be this." Now, I am not a cutter or a draper, but I can envision things, and I'm not afraid to try things, even if they're not perfect.

A lightbulb went off as we waited for Shonda to join us by video, and I started to wrap the dress, overlaying it with transparent tulle. I then put a huge flower on the shoulder. It was somewhat impressionistic in its feel, and it was in that moment that the blurred lines of *Bridgerton* were truly born.

"*We had to stage an incredible amount of costumes. It cost a fortune to build a wardrobe: Ellen Mirojnick had a right merry time and would spend eighty thousand here and there on material. As the invoices came in, we'd say, 'Oh, there goes Ellen, shopping again!' The factory ultimately held eighteen hundred dresses, all cataloged. Phoebe alone had eighty-six dresses.*"

—Sarada McDermott

Betsy and Shonda
on Corseting as Metaphor

SHONDA: Corsets were a central piece of visual language in *Bridgerton* simply because they are a perfect metaphor for the times and the constraints placed on women—physically, certainly, it's hard to breathe and move in a corset!—but also the idea that society should restrain your flesh and dictate where it should be.

BETSY: They are the opposite of liberating. Nicola Coughlan also made the brilliant observation that you can't put a corset on by yourself. This points not only to social status—you needed to have helping hands to strap you in—but also to this idea that a corset was something put on you. It impedes every woman's agency, transforming them from actors into objects.

SHONDA: Ellen Mirojnick talks about how corsets were designed to accentuate the waist, obviously, but really, the goal was to create a female shape that was like a vessel, or vase, with the bosom flowering out the top. It's the epitome of objectification.

BETSY: Yes, and it's mirrored in that great exchange between Eloise and Penelope at the gallery, when they're looking at a painting of water nymphs. Eloise says something to the effect of: "Like all paintings by men, he sees a woman as nothing more than a decorative object." And Penelope confirms that they are depicted as "human vases." You can obviously pull that idea out to its natural conclusion: In Regency England, women were objectified vessels for carrying babies. It's not very comforting!

DR. HANNAH GREIG ON THE COLORS AND DRESSES OF THE DAY:

People will find many of the colors in *Bridgerton* quite surprising, but it's important to remember that when we see materials from the era in museums, they're two hundred years old: They're often faded and antiqued. You really have to use your imagination to think of what the clothing would have looked like, brand-new and sparkling in candlelight.

What's more, museums have tended to collect things that are regarded as tasteful at the time they were collected—it's easy to forget how this informs the way in which we imagine our history. Over time, bad aesthetics are filtered out, defining entire periods. Many of the color combinations in the show are a classic Regency palette—the pale shades, the white and cream dresses, pretty much the entire *Bridgerton* closet is very much in keeping with the aesthetics of the time. The slightly more gaudy schemes of the Featheringtons might seem off the scale and improbable, but those types of fabrics capture the spirit of those who followed a different fashion, were out of fashion, or perhaps just got their fashions wrong.

Bridgerton also gets something else right that many period dramas get wrong: The Technicolor world in *Bridgerton* includes other social classes. I get quite frustrated when we see people of lower social classes and servants look really shabby and plain on-screen. Fashion was not solely the provenance of the uber-rich—just as now, it came at various price points. Domestic maids and young women were famously fashionable as well, along with actresses and other women who managed to attain celebrity status; the aristocrats weren't the only ones who could dress to impress.

Ellen on Costuming the Ton

Costuming Daphne:

Daphne is the only character in the series who has so much simplicity in her costume design—we wanted to keep the lines and palette as elegant and refined as possible.

Because of this, there's practically no adornment at all—just color and shape and Daphne! Her accessories are tiny, nothing is overdone or overblown. She's just a breath of beauty. And her hair and makeup were designed to channel Audrey Hepburn in *War and Peace*. Her ball gowns are stoned and embellished by hand, and each one has a different design—but it's very subtle. It's pretty difficult to achieve this, to be honest, because you want the cut of the clothes and the movement to be divine.

As she evolves and matures, she is no longer a porcelain doll—she becomes a mature woman, which we achieve simply by shifting the color toward more dusky, richer tones. We didn't want her to look older—after all, she's not older—but she does become more worldly through her relationship with Simon, and we wanted to reflect that in the clothing, just as it was subtly reflected in the makeup and the hair.

"It's funny looking back at early versions, because we really reimagined Daphne. At first she had aspirations of attending Oxford and then had to put those dreams down to enter the marriage mart as the dutiful oldest daughter. (Those aspirations would later be given to Eloise.) But in those early days, Chris realized it would be way more fun if you had a girl who didn't have to suppress her desires and was ready for her moment in the marriage mart—a girl so perfect and primed for landing her love match that when it goes south in slow dawning terror, it would really carry the story forward."

—Alison Eakle

Costuming Lady Featherington:

The goal was to convey that because Lady Featherington does not inherently have status, she feels she needs to telegraph it through the opulence of her dress. The Featheringtons are new money, and they want to fit in. Ironically, Lady Featherington only knows how to do that by standing out and drawing as much attention to herself and her daughters as possible.

In that time period, women of that status changed their clothes four or even five times a day. You got up and changed into your morning dress; then there was the day dress; the tea dress; then the dinner dress. And, of course, there were gowns for the ball, and maybe even another dress in between.

So when Lady Featherington says she needs ten more dresses, she really means it: You could not wear the same dress twice. At that level of society, you would never want to give any inkling that you might not have enough money.

Costuming the Queen:

Golda Rosheuvel came into our first fitting with a soul filled with passion and a spirit filled with raw energy. Her eyes lit up with anticipation and raw mischief. Honestly, she had left Golda on the other side of the door and was already in the process of transforming into Queen Charlotte. It was thrilling to be in the room with her.

Golda was all in for anything we wanted to do. The thing about Golda is that she could carry anything we created for her. Her electricity inspired and informed every color combination, silk, and embellishment that we could imagine. Golda lit up Queen Charlotte like a firefly.

"Golda wears the court dress as Queen Charlotte—these big, wide hooped skirts—which were actually a throwback to an earlier eighteenth-century style. Historically, the queen did not dress for the period with an Empire waist, the fashion of the day: Her whole court adhered to the dress code of the 1780s. What I found on set was that Golda's dresses were so wide that they forced a space around her—no one could get close or brush up against her. She is set apart by her costume, and you literally have to stand back and keep your distance. As a historian, I always love those moments on set where you suddenly understand the power of costume—and how intimidating it could be, as women's clothing had a real, physical effect."

—Dr. Hannah Greig

DR. HANNAH GREIG ON THE JEWELRY OF THE DAY:

Ellen and John used copious amounts of jewelry and accessories in *Bridgerton*—instead of taking things off, they just kept putting more and more on. The idea of bling really captures the energy of the time and what society at the time was focused on: It was very, very showy. Members of the ton wore jewelry with *everything*. This includes the men, who would have jewel buttons on their jackets and diamonds set into their snuff boxes and pocket watches and the hilts of their sword. In *Bridgerton*, the Duke of Hastings wears a brooch in almost every scene—I believe it was his mother's brooch. As a historian, I've always been interested in how bejeweled the period was—this was the first time I saw it fully brought to life on-screen.

As we know, butterflies (Featheringtons) and bees (Bridgertons) show up throughout the *Bridgerton* series to symbolize the two families. The idea of working your family's lineage into your dress and accessories was not uncommon at the time.

"We designed our principal jewelry, creating tiaras, hairpieces, necklaces and rings, and more, based on historical pieces. We wanted the feeling of large over-the-top luxury. Lorenzo Mancianti would interpret and sculpt them according to the color of gems that we wanted."

—Ellen Mirojnick

Costuming Lady Danbury:

"Lady Danbury can do what she likes and go where she likes and have whatever kind of London life she likes. She is a wealthy widow with the title, money, and freedom to do as she pleases. Her costumes broadcast that: a sharp hat, a tailored jacket, the stick that she carries with style and authority. Through her costume and her stance, we usually see her demanding the room's attention, as if the commander of a regiment."

—Dr. Hannah Greig

"I wanted clean lines, and a hat, and a cane, and a fag for Lady Danbury, because she's a widow and fully in her masculine—there's something about her that suggests she knows where Bohemian land is. She would be hanging out with Benedict and the artists. She's friends with Lucy and Henry Granville. She knows the secrets. She's seen all sides of the street, and she's unfazed."

—Adjoa Andoh

Costuming Penelope:

Nicola was one of the first people cast, and we had her come in so we could photograph her in different yellows, greens, and oranges to determine what citrus colors she could wear comfortably—while the Featheringtons are "funny," we didn't want her to look tacky, as she's a serious character. We also had to take her red wigs into consideration.

If you look closely, you'll see that for her first ball, we had the amazing craftspeople and artisans in our studio hand-embroider and Swarovski-stone her dress with a beautiful butterfly across the bodice. It was a juicy citrus, and it was stunning. And for Vauxhall, she wears a butterfly necklace and a beautiful pink dress—as she tells Colin, she was only allowed to wear something not orange or yellow because her mom was not in attendance.

Costuming Eloise:

Eloise refuses to be girlie—in fact, she resents nothing more in the world than this idea that she should dress up like a girl. And throughout the first season, she refuses to drop her hem—because she recognizes that the moment her hem drops, she'll have to take her turn in the marriage mart.

She is buttoned up to her neck and has no interest in exposing herself in any way. We added subtly masculine details, like shirting with a shadow stripe that we paired with something a bit more sheer to make it appropriately feminine. We made her a jacket that looked like a men's cutaway coat. And then we left the rest to her body language, her gait, and the way she is forceful in the way she moves.

Her hair is also telling—the Regency-era mullet was actually a popular haircut at the time, since the age was Grecian-inspired. Marc Pilcher chose the look for her because she was a tomboy, feminist, more rough-and-tumble—it's just messier and more unkempt than the other girls but actually period-appropriate.

Season 2 Costume Designer Sophie Canale:

In Season 2, Eloise's sister Daphne is now the Duchess of Hastings and can be seen in lilacs, so you'll see Eloise on occasion wearing Bridgerton blue, representing the family color. Fabric choices are incredibly important to me for defining a character. With Eloise's day wear, I intentionally used stripes, checks, and small self-patterned fabrics, which provide a more masculine look than the floral fabrics of the ton. Since Eloise is now a debutante, I also wanted to create a slightly softer look for her. I used softer fabrics such as silk chiffons. We also added details of ribbons, small jewelry, hairpins, and brooches. Her true transformation is her ball and evening wear, which can be seen in her blue ball gown, worn for her first ball of the season.

Ellen Mirojnick on Costuming the Men:

We wanted the men to look really fashionable, which can be hard in a Regency style, and so we broke some conventions. For example, not every man can wear white trousers—except for Anthony. Anthony wore the white pants, he felt them, he understood them, and they looked right. But they did not work for Simon, even though Simon was rare in that he could wear period and it suited him perfectly. So while many of the pants on the men *look* period, they're not actually period; we constructed them in a different way and changed the colors. We wanted our men to look as handsome as possible.

Simon traveled before coming back to London, and we wanted to represent that through trinkets from afar. He was also not interested in what people thought of him, nor did he grow up with other people looking over his shoulder. We didn't want to tie him up through the neck with a stock and make him formal. We gave him a casual independence by opening up his shirt collar and often putting a scarf inside.

This could have looked too pretentious or not correct, but it worked perfectly because he could pull it off. We also took liberties and gave him different colors that wouldn't have been the convention at that time. If we had constrained him by all of the details of the period, it wouldn't have felt natural on him, and we wanted him to feel real.

Costuming Marina:

We wanted to telegraph that Marina is different—softer, from the country, more natural. You'll notice that she is one of the only girls in the marriage mart who wears small prints. And even as her dresses start to evolve to look more like the Featheringtons', it was really in color only—she still stands apart, the fabrics are more touchable. For hair and makeup, they also wanted to maintain that feeling of freshness. Her hair is loose and natural, not too coiffed.

Costuming the Modiste:

When Kathryn first came in for the fitting, she wanted more colorful clothes, dresses to match or rival the ones that she herself made for the society ladies. But we felt strongly that she would wear black, much like Coco Chanel, to set herself apart from the fashion trends that she was creating, that she would be defining style in part by not being "in style."

Within *Bridgerton*, it is a brilliant conceit to have the women gather and gossip at Madame Delacroix's shop—it's a way for them to run into each other and storylines to collide. But in reality, she would have visited these women in their homes, and there would have been runners bringing swaths of fabric across town to show the ladies for approval.

Sophie Canale on the Sharmas:

We had a big discussion with the showrunner and producer about how to represent the Sharma family using Regency dresses. We ended up using Indian fabrics and Indian embroidery. The jewel-tone color palettes of Kate Sharma's costumes are important, and all the family's jewelry is Indian-inspired. Even though they're in Empire-line dresses, there are still elements of their heritage throughout. For the jewelry, the Bridgertons tend to be in silver, the Featheringtons, gold, and for the Sharmas, rose gold.

Charithra Chandran on Edwina's Evolution:

When I went to the first costume fitting, I was actually very emotional—plus, pink is my favorite color, and so the fact that it was Edwina's color was exciting to me. If you ask every character, each one feels like her costumes are the best, and that's because they so perfectly fit our characters.

At the beginning of the season, Edwina's got big, curly hair and very rosy cheeks and doe eyes. As the season progresses and she gets wiser and heartbroken, her entire look changes and deepens. Her costumes and hair and makeup drastically evolve, and her voice changes. In the first two episodes, she's very softly spoken and like a fairy, like she's putting on a part—but as she becomes increasingly disillusioned with the world and the people around her, her voice drops. It becomes more coarse as she stops wanting to pretend.

Historian Dr. Hannah Greig on Servant Livery:

While the color-matching that we see in *Bridgerton* between the houses, the families, and the servants is very pronounced as a visual language for tying the worlds together, it is tethered in the reality of Regency England. Aristocratic families in London typically dressed their servants in one livery and one color of uniform, so you could spot your theme on the street easily. And if we're honest, it was also so other people could spot your servants in the street—it was a way of broadcasting status.

While Will Hughes-Jones talks about matching the livery to the interior so that the servants can fade into the wallpaper, at the time, the uniform of the servants would not have necessarily been designed to blend in simply because people would not have noticed their presence as much as we would today. In the high-society Regency world, they are used to being surrounded by people all the time, which is no longer our experience. When it comes to filming, they needed to be relatively disguised, because having a man standing in the doorway can be distracting for the viewer, particularly since we're so unused to seeing people in a familial space.

WEDDINGS

DR. HANNAH GREIG ON CHILL REGENCY WEDDINGS:

In Regency England, weddings were subdued and private: Your family would be in attendance, you might wear a new dress (particularly if you're a Bridgerton!), and you would exchange rings, but it would be an understated piece of jewelry, like what we see Simon give Daphne. The wedding banquet, too, was a *Bridgerton* construct—the show is a fantasy, not a documentary, after all! A three-tier wedding cake wouldn't have been baked, but I did love the conversation between the staff about the sugar shortage and whiteness of the cake: That was all accurate. Sugar was very precious and rare, and a pristine white cake would have been a sight indeed.

Engagements were also not long. After arranging the contract to marriage—the dowry and all of those other deeply unromantic details—you would "publish" your "banns," or post them, essentially, a few weeks in advance, in public, at the church. This proclamation of your intent to marry would give people the opportunity to complain, protest, or stop the alliance. This was about protecting estates: ensuring daughters didn't run off with footmen, that everyone's honor was, in fact, intact and nobody could stake a claim to the title. The only place where you could lawfully wed without publishing banns was Gretna Green, in Scotland, where Marina and Colin intend to elope. In *Bridgerton*, by granting a special license, Queen Charlotte permitted the future duke and duchess to marry without bothering with banns, ensuring that Cressida Cowper didn't have a chance to start a whisper campaign about Daphne's virtue. Though it wasn't exactly historically accurate, we can't blame the Bridgertons for using the opportunity to throw a great party.

TOM VERICA ON THE EDWINA-ANTHONY WEDDING:

We wanted to strike the balance between historical accuracy—Regency-era weddings were typically small family affairs—while making it accessible for a modern viewer. And there were a lot of things that were spot on: The queen was hosting, for her own entertainment, and it was clearly her intention to have the full ton present to witness the event. She wanted a front-row seat, along with all the theatrics. It's not what she was expecting, but she is always trying to create a spectacle. It had to be a very big, very public event.

I'm always looking for little moments and elements and nods, and I wanted to use similar imagery to Season 1, when Simon and Daphne's hands almost touch in front of the painting. So you'll notice that when Anthony walks in and passes Kate, to do his duty and be with his bride, there's a similar element of two people yearning to be together.

After Edwina becomes a runaway bride and has her very public revelation, there were a lot of great elements. Chris Van Dusen writes beautiful moments that are vulnerable, cutting, and punishing. Right after the wedding, Edwina corrects Kate: "Half sister." This episode and event were really the education of Edwina, and her growing up and finding her voice, and taking ownership and power over who she is.

When King George walks into the room, I think there's a recognition of the history of love between these two people. Edwina sees the connection between the king and the queen and his fragility in that moment. And part of her gaining her voice is stepping in in an instinctual way to take care of someone, to calm the situation. It's a very spontaneous moment from someone who is showing that she can be an adult. Edwina takes the lead. It's a moment of discovery for a lot of people who see her do that.

CHARITHRA CHANDRAN ON THE WEDDING SCENE:

That was a very scary scene to film because there were hundreds of supporting artists, and it all happened in real time. The scene is long—it begins with Edwina walking down the aisle and ends when she turns to run back down the aisle—and so filming it felt very real and very high-stakes.

And ultimately, she's experiencing a huge betrayal. By the end of the episode, she thinks Anthony is trash and that she can do much better than him, but she's destroyed by her sister. This isn't about a man, it's about the love between two sisters, soulmates, really. They are experiencing a breakup, and that's the painful part. And there are no villains, really. You can't look at Anthony and Kate and think they're bad. That's why the show is so great, we are all really nuanced characters.

After, when the king comes into Queen Charlotte's chambers and they're sitting there, in Edwina's mind, she just sees a man who is struggling. She wants to end his pain and make the king and queen feel a bit better.

SIMONE ASHLEY ON THE WEDDING SCENE:

When we meet Kate, she's this extremely fierce, hard-core tough cookie, but by the wedding, you see that break down a bit. She's incredibly vulnerable and soft, and you see it comes from a place of her being too afraid to do what she wants; she's so used to taking care of the people around her. Anthony finds her in a closet, where he grabs her, and is like, "Can we just take a moment and talk about what's happening?" But she's very scared and runs away.

Production Design

"Even though he says he was okay with breaking some rules, Will Hughes-Jones was obsessive about period detail. Fortunately, no moments of modernity wound up in my shots (though we did occasionally have to reshoot outdoor scenes when a plane would fly overhead). But I really credit Will, because he wouldn't allow anything non-Regency onto the set. He would also get the on-set art director, David Crewdson, to dress in orange. If there was something Will didn't like, if there was a roof he didn't like, David would stand there without moving. We would know that we couldn't move the camera to the point where a guy is standing there dressed in bright orange. It was actually a brilliant trick!"

—Julie Anne Robinson

SET DECORATOR GINA CROMWELL:

When Will Hughes-Jones first called me about the job, he was quite vague: I heard Netflix, Shondaland, Regency, colorful, bright, fast, and exciting. His first pitch was effectively, "It's like the Kennedys versus the Kardashians." The classic old-money Bridgertons and the nouveau-riche Featheringtons.

The producers stressed that they wanted everything to look new, as it would have been in those days, which is interesting, because when you are dressing period sets, you always have an inner conflict in your head that it looks weird if it's too new. That's because when we see things that have patina and wear and tear on them, modern viewers think, "Period." We think that's what gives them their charm.

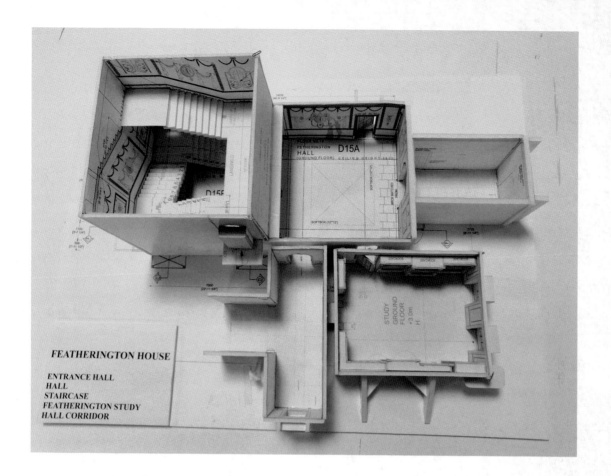

FEATHERINGTON HOUSE

ENTRANCE HALL
HALL
STAIRCASE
FEATHERINGTON STUDY
HALL CORRIDOR

WILL HUGHES JONES: We took the moodboards that Ellen was working on for costumes and juxtaposed them with the locations and came up with a formula for building what we knew we would need. With Chris Van Dusen reminding us that he wanted the show to have a heightened look to it, we dialed it up an extra 20 percent in color, richness, and scale.

Once we determined the family palettes, we continued to have creative conversations with everyone, including Jeff Jur, the director of photography, because with his lighting, he was responsible for the overall tone of the piece. Once you start shooting, the train has really left the station, and you all need to stick with the plan. If you find yourself needing to make big changes midproduction, it can really diminish the desired effect.

The upside of it being a train, though, is that you have somewhat of a predetermined track—there was a lot of trust involved, but the team knew how to realize the vision of the writers. And we did have CGI [computer-generated imagery] to catch us if we fell, though I'm very much a person who likes to design sets that you can physically see. I don't like to rely on post-production, it's absolutely the last line of defense. This is not to say that we didn't need a little help now and then, because Regency doesn't exist in the twenty-first century, so they had a fair amount of work to do to tidy the edges. Clyvedon Village was a good example of doing as much work as possible to eliminate modernity, but we couldn't remove electricity!

Anatomy of a Scene
CLYVEDON VILLAGE

DIRECTOR: JULIE ANNE ROBINSON • EPISODE: 106—"SWISH"

WILL HUGHES-JONES ON BRINGING CLYVEDON VILLAGE TO LIFE:

We used Castle Howard as a stand-in for the fictional Clyvedon, the Duke of Hasting's estate—and relatedly, we used the village of Coneysthorpe, which is the estate village of Castle Howard, as Clyvedon Village. So a one-to-one swap across the board. Everyone who lives in Coneysthorpe today is connected to the Castle Howard estate, much as Clyvedon Village inhabitants would have been connected to Clyvedon. The estate owns all the land, and the farmers are tenants. There's a tithe relationship with expectations on both sides: The landlords are expected to look after the estate and show up at the local events and host the community—they are supposed to play a good paternalistic role. People would certainly express their displeasure if this didn't happen. You get the sense that Simon is very much neglecting his duty as estate owner in the show. You learn that things aren't as they should be, and there are rippling tensions when he first encounters people at the fair.

Coneysthorpe still looks and feels like it would have in the period, though obviously, it's been modernized over the decades, so we needed to roll back time a bit. We had twelve people over four days changing all the windows into the color and shape that we see in the show—and those people stayed behind to turn them all back. We took down white picket fences and put up a wall to block the view of traffic at the bottom of the hill, and we reroofed Joanna's cottage—the villager who befriends Daphne—to make it look period-appropriate. We wanted to be respectful of the village and people living there, and so we used local stone and materials as much as possible as we worked. Where we couldn't, we covered surfaces in black foil and painted it to look like stone. Occasionally, it becomes a toss-up between us physically disguising moments of modernity or having the CGI team paint them out: We couldn't remove the TV aerials, so those were removed in post-production.

GINA CROMWELL ON DECORATING THE VILLAGE SQUARE:

There were about seventy people in this scene, including in-action carriages and carts, donkeys, horses, cows, sheep, goats, and pigs. Typically, the set decoration team will do a plan in advance so that we have a blueprint of what we need and where it needs to go; then we load up the lorries and cart in the set dressing. For the village fair, we obviously had to have a beer tent—it's an English show! And we wanted to continue the thematic of the flowers because *Bridgerton* is so bright and beautiful, so we added carts full of dried flowers, since Clyvedon Village is a more rustic set. At the time, farmers would have come in for the fair and then spent the day sitting on their carts. We deployed these strategically, and it was useful, as it gave the set some height, too.

GINA CROMWELL ON STARTING OVER AND HITTING THE RIGHT NOTES:

The first thing we did was to visit with the costume team to see how they were approaching the design—we needed to understand the palette so that our sets would complement their work. Blues, creams, and violets for the Bridgertons, while the Featheringtons were acidic greens, yellows, and peachy orange colors. The costumers were quite influenced by a big exhibition in London about Christian Dior, which was quite interesting, as we had a book called *Dior and His Decorators*, and it had this feel to it that gave us a good mash-up perspective on the Regency period we were trying to represent.

The Featheringtons were trickier, for sure, and it took us a long time to figure out how to crack that nut. We decided to go with a look inspired by a very, very fashionable designer from the times who was getting inspiration from Egypt as well as Greece and Rome. We found chairs with sphinxes on the arms, and if you look carefully, you'll see we had panthers up on the curtain pole. When it came to the drapes, which were a big deal, we focused on a collection of catalogs put together by Rudolph Ackermann.

GINA CROMWELL ON MOODBOARDING AND 1815 VEGAS:

Moodboards are absolutely critical to the process, because Will Hughes-Jones and I might have a shorthand, but we need to be able to communicate our vision to everyone else. Typically, we start with references—historical paintings and other elements that we know to be correct. And then to give a sense of mood, we'll pull from magazines or more modern environments to suggest the essence of what we want to create in the space.

In Season 2, there's the club that we designed—Chris described it to Will as wanting it to be like Vegas. So you take a deep breath and think, "Okay, how do we do Vegas in 1815?" Will knew about a building called Spencer House in London that has these palm trees made of plaster. I looked back at the photo that Chris had sent for inspiration and thought, "Well, this Vegas place has palm trees, plants, and lots of different colors." And it really did inspire what we did for that club, it illustrated the atmosphere that we needed to create.

I think it's important to know your period because then you know how you can stretch it. It's quite liberating once you decide not to back yourself into a corner by making everything absolutely bang-on correct. Sometimes you need to pick something that gives you the right feel without looking strikingly out of place and that might not be accurate. We were certainly given permission to do that on *Bridgerton*.

Anatomy of a Scene
VAUXHALL PLEASURE GARDENS

DIRECTOR: JULIE ANNE ROBINSON • EPISODE: 101—"DIAMOND OF THE FIRST WATER"

LOCATION: Temple Of Venus, Stowe House, Buckinghamshire

KEY SONG: "We Could Form An Attachment" by Kris Bowers

BEST LINE: "With you on my arm, the world will believe I have finally found my duchess. Every presumptuous mother in town will leave me alone. And every suitor will be looking *at you*. You must know men are always interested in a woman if they believe another, particularly a duke, to be interested as well." —DUKE OF HASTINGS

KEY OCCURRENCE: Daphne and Simon establish their ruse, and Daphne plants a facer on Nigel Berbrooke.

CAST: Principles, plus 170 supporting artists, including 6 Vauxhall sellers, 4 Pandean minstrels, 10 Vauxhall musicians, 1 master of ceremonies.

CREW: Principles, plus 16 horses, 7 SFX technicians, 2 assistant directors, 5 crowd runners, 2 choreographers, 5 camera operators, 3 drone operators, 10 electrical, 4 grips, 16 security, 54 costumers, 26 hair-and-makeup artists, 2 sound engineers, 1 VFX supervisor, 1 script supervisor, 2 medics, 1 dialect coach, 1 etiquette adviser, 1 intimacy coordinator

DR. HANNAH GREIG ON THE VAUXHALL PLEASURE GARDENS: I've never been involved in a filming of the scale of this scene, but it was simply incredible—to be outdoors in the elements on a warm summer's evening, watching something that so closely replicated what it must have been like in Regency England. The lighting, and the fireworks, and the music, and the food, and the dancing: It was a real party. The Pleasure Gardens were a major cultural touchstone, and as a historian, it felt like the closest I would ever get to experiencing anything like it.

There's a lovely image of the Vauxhall Pleasure Gardens from the 1780s or so that shows London society crowded around the orchestra area of Vauxhall, and you can see many of the celebrities of the day. Around them, you see the rest of London society and then different social classes watching. And over behind a couple of trees, you'll see newspaper editors spying on them for their columns the next day. It feels just like *Bridgerton*.

WILL HUGHES-JONES:
In the period, the trees were lit up by lamps filled with whale oil—which smelled dreadful, so the Pleasure Gardens would have absolutely stank. Through research, we surmised that they were likely polished globes to reflect light back, so we installed two and a half kilometers of lighting and then buried all the cords under additional plots of lawn. (Christmas came early for one bulb manufacturer, because we bought twenty-five hundred bulbs to cover all of our buildings.) We built a bandstand for the orchestra, and food was served below. And then we set up three hundred towers with open flames to line the walkway.

"The Vauxhall Pleasure Gardens were public: If you could pay your penny, you could go, which means you get a very different crowd and a very different vibe. We have it in the first episode in contrast to Lady Danbury's invited ball. It makes the whole thing so exciting. You can imagine, at the time, how it would feel new and inspire curiosity, the experience that we all want to have at that age."

—Jack Murphy

Perhaps most pointedly, the pyrotechnics team got to have a lot of fun: We built these huge stands, and then they individually wired each firework so the team could program them and remote-control the entire operation off camera. When the night sky is lit up by fireworks as Daphne and Simon dance for the first time, it's probably one of the most memorable scenes of the entire season. All of those fireworks—save for about six, which were way up in the sky and placed by CGI—were real.

It definitely made for beautiful TV, though I think we got it quite close to what it would have been like in the period. But we're not making a history show. As long as it doesn't take you away from the drama, we feel like we've won.

INTIMACY COORDINATOR LIZZY TALBOT:
In this society, most touching is forbidden, at least for the women. Even though this world is ruled by restraint, there are still those moments of break-through, of modern flirting tactics: little smiles and laughs, head tosses, knowing looks. Members of the ton really nailed the eye contact.

The balls were critical because they're one of the occasions where all of these people are assembled together, in one room, and they are trying to figure out who they are going to marry—the stakes are major. It's like Tinder or speed dating, but you go straight to the altar without ever being alone together.

But they can dance (hopefully more than once). When they're dancing, they're holding each other for the first time and feeling each other's bodies just a little bit. Their hands—not bare—are touching. It is their chance to gauge chemistry, to have a conversation while they're trying to make the biggest decision of their lives. It really makes these moments loaded with innuendo, and we worked hard to telegraph that—the thirst, the sexiness, the unspoken desire.

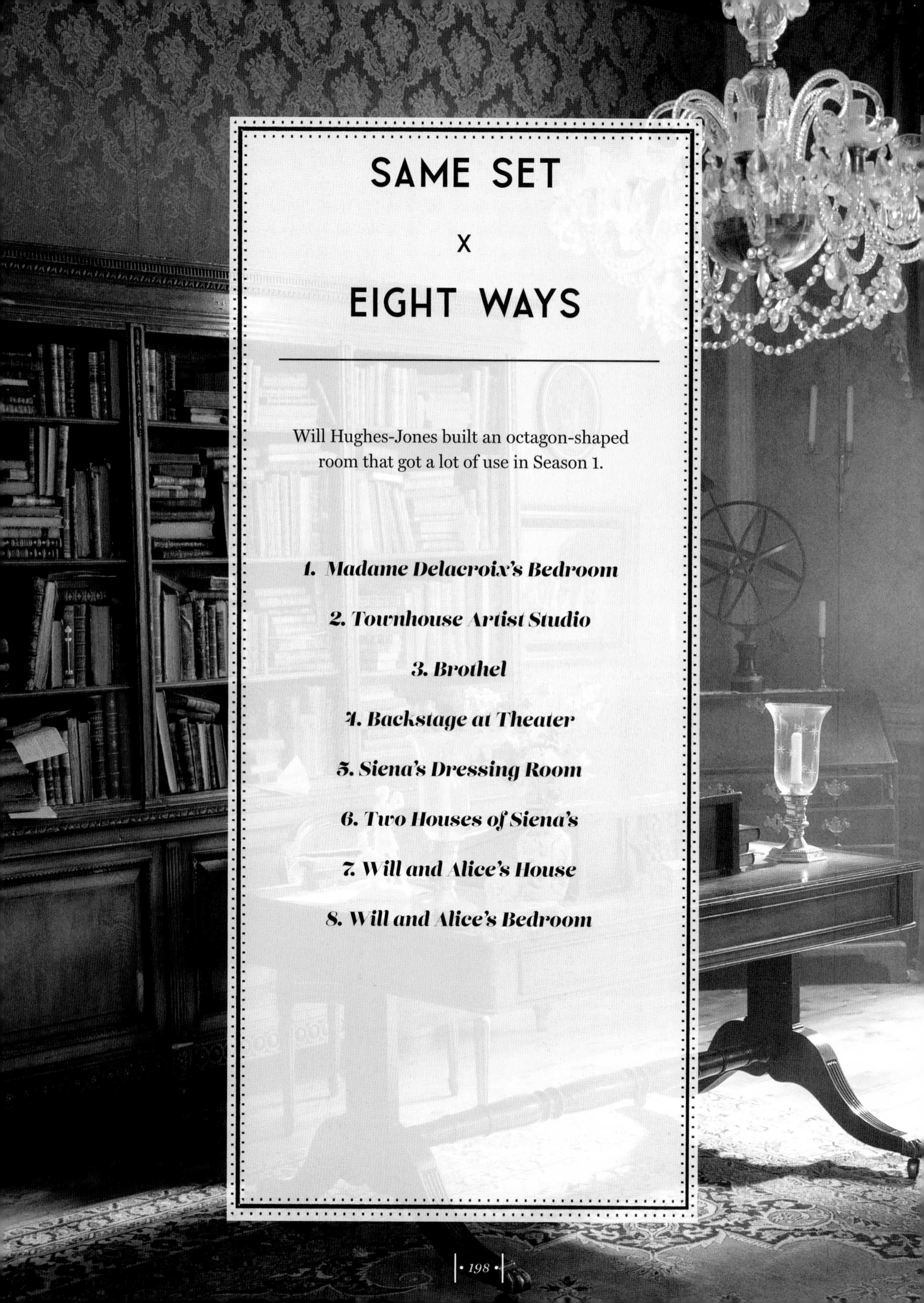

SAME SET

x

EIGHT WAYS

Will Hughes-Jones built an octagon-shaped room that got a lot of use in Season 1.

1. *Madame Delacroix's Bedroom*

2. *Townhouse Artist Studio*

3. *Brothel*

4. *Backstage at Theater*

5. *Siena's Dressing Room*

6. *Two Houses of Siena's*

7. *Will and Alice's House*

8. *Will and Alice's Bedroom*

GINA ON HER FAVORITE ROOMS:
I absolutely love designing kitchens, the Bridgerton kitchen in particular. I loved that scene when Anthony and Daphne go downstairs to warm up some milk, and they're just staring blankly at this old iron stove with absolutely no clue how to get it going. Chris told us that he wanted it to look really complicated, with all sorts of knobs and levers. And, of course, I thought, "What knobs and levers? They didn't have knobs and levers." I mean, they literally put a fire in it and then hung chains down. So we tried to figure out how to make it seem more complicated with extra knobs and hooks.

We also all really loved the artists' studio, which, regretfully, we didn't get to see as much as we would have liked in Season 1. Fortunately, the writers brought it back in Season 2 in a big way.

We had one really special afternoon as a team in the artists' studio, before we filmed the scene with Benedict in Season 1. The life-artist models came in and posed and we drew them. Everyone on the team has been to art college, and we used to do that all the time, but I hadn't done it in decades. So we just stopped running around, and sat there in silence, and drew the models. It was really, really lovely, a nice treat amongst the chaos.

WILL ON MAKING SUMMER IN DECEMBER:

The queen's party in Season 1 takes place in summer, but we shot this in December, after a very hard frost, and it was *cold*. First we had to blowtorch the ground because it was completely frozen. All of the actors were in silk shoes, and so the costume team asked if we could protect the footwear, so we laid down Astroturf everywhere. Then we needed to put hedges all the way around to hide the view because all of the beech trees had no leaves on them. And then we had to wire plastic blossoms onto the existing trees to make them look like trees in bloom. When Daphne goes off to a side garden to speak to her mother, there was a large wall with dead ivy, and so we used the wisteria from the Bridgerton House facade to make it look bright and alive again.

It was a huge undertaking for us but also for everyone else. Jeff Jur had to light it to look like a beautiful summer day and then keep the cameras from going above the hedges, because the oak trees in the distance were denuded. The costume team had to keep all the actors warm because they were wearing flimsy dresses and it was hovering just above zero. It was also windy and rainy, so the hair and makeup team were hustling to keep everyone looking beautiful through this miserable couple of days. I think it was the most impressive collaborative moment in the show where we all hunkered down and made it happen.

Anatomy of a Scene
TROWBRIDGE BALL

DIRECTOR: SHEREE FOLKSON • EPISODE: 104–"AN AFFAIR OF HONOR"

DR. HANNAH GREIG ON THE HISTORICAL ACCURACY OF THE TROWBRIDGE BALL:

We shot the Trowbridge Ball at Hatfield House in Hertfordshire, which was built in 1611 by Robert Cecil, the First Earl of Salisbury and chief minister to King James I (it is currently the home of the Seventh Marquess of Salisbury). It is an incredible country house with innumerable grand state rooms and gardens, really the perfect backdrop to the opulence of this particular scene. I think they were expecting me to go onto the set and wag my finger and say, "This is not historically accurate at all," but actually, it was. The fashionable world certainly knew how to put on a party and frequently created very elaborate and ornate set designs for their events—they hired dancers, acrobats, performers. This ball really captured the excessiveness of the period, the passion for extravagance, the impulse to flex wealth, and a desire to be entertained. They weren't going to see me have a historian meltdown. And not even cross-dressing could cause that. Because within the beau monde, people frequently played with identity: Men dressed as women, women dressed as men. This was part and parcel of social life.

**JACK MURPHY ON BREAKING
HISTORICAL PRECEDENTS:**

When I was choreographing, I would first put everything to period music, then I would put it to modern music. And then they placed the score over it at the end. For the Trowbridge Ball, I put on the song "Blurred Lines"—without any lyrics so as not to offend anyone—because I wanted something with soul and energy that would allow me to realize the world historically while finding polarity in the fantasy. And at the Trowbridge Ball, they dance to a cha-cha-cha and a samba—but the rhythm is so close, and the music works, that it's barely perceptible. It's my little secret from you all—except for all those viewers in Brazil!

WILL HUGHES-JONES
ON THE FOOD STYLING:

For the balls and parties, it very much became about the architecture for my team: how tall can we build a macaroon tower, for example. We always needed elements with real height and color so that we could infuse the rooms with texture and brightness. Sometimes it was a tower of strawberries, or champagne flutes, or cakes. One of our home economists created a whole display around a swan with pies, loads of amazing fruits, and red currants.

I wasn't expecting to be doing that much food, so it became a running joke, because every time I'd ask Chris what he wanted to see at the balls, his answer was: "Food! Food and lots and lots of flowers."

Using the Real Regency England

BADMINTON HOUSE
LOCATION: Gloucestershire
USED FOR: Den of Iniquity

WILTON HOUSE
LOCATION: Salisbury
USED FOR: Many of the queen's scenes, including the Presentation Scene

CASTLE HOWARD
LOCATION: Yorkshire
USED FOR: Clyvedon Castle

LANCASTER HOUSE
LOCATION: London
USED FOR: Violet's visit to the queen for tea

BERKSHIRE POLO CLUB
LOCATION: Cranbourne
USED FOR: The racetrack.

SYON HOUSE
LOCATION: Brentford
USED FOR: The conservatory ballroom.

WROTHAM PARK
LOCATION: Hertfordshire
USED FOR: The Bridgerton's country estate, Aubrey Hall

HAMPTON COURT
LOCATION: Molesley
USED FOR: Buckingham House, the Queen's residence, where Edwina and Anthony are supposed to wed.

WILTON HOUSE
LOCATION: Salisbury
USED FOR: Presentation Day, and where the Queen and Lady Danbury have tea.

SARA FISCHER ON THE "LOCATION PORN" THAT MADE UP THE WORLD OF *BRIDGERTON*:
Every location was more jaw-dropping than the next. You'd get to a "house," and it might be on ten thousand acres and have ninety-seven rooms. Then you're on to the next, which could be three times as large. It is a wild and grand world. But even though we saw some incredible properties in England, I still think that the sets Will Hughes-Jones built by hand were some of the most stunning pieces of scenery in the show.

PRODUCTION DESIGNER WILL HUGHES-JONES ON THE NIGHTMARE OF LOGISTICS:
Building sets is one animal, but being on location is another kind of beast: Not only do you have to create worlds on locations, but then you have to pack it all down and return it to the owners the way you found it. We had crews at all locations days before and days after, doing this work.

One day we were in seven locations: That was a hideous day. But on any normal day, we have lorries traveling across the country and were filling our cars and driving set dressing or artificial flowers to locations.

Our amazing prop master, Noel Cowell, and his team managed most of the transport, getting things from A to B and making sure that everything is where it needs to be at the right time.

You can imagine our calendars with Post-it Notes—everything being moved around on a daily basis.

SET DECORATOR GINA CROMWELL ON
TRANSFORMING TOUGH LOCATIONS:

The Season 2 racecourse was a big job, particularly when Will turned to me and asked, "Can you cover that entire building with fabric, please?" We had to turn a pavilion, quite a modern one, into what looked like a Regency tent for the queen. Thank goodness it wasn't windy!

I also loved creating the theater. It's exciting when you go to a location that's not period-correct and you need to problem-solve and figure out how to make it work.

In that case, it was a massive job, and we struggled to find a theatrical painter who could paint a scenic backdrop and the wings on time. Everything had to be measured so it would fit perfectly, and the canvases were laid out on the floor to be painted. Will and I were sitting on another location, having just finished dressing that set, when they sent through pictures of the wings and backdrops installed. We cried because it worked so perfectly.

Anatomy of a Scene
HASTINGS BALL

DIRECTOR: ALRICK RILEY • EPISODE: 108—"AFTER THE RAIN"

LOCATION:
Hand-Built Set

KEY SONGS:
"The Four Seasons"
by Antonio Vivaldi,
recomposed by
Max Richter

BEST LINE:
"Just because something
is not perfect does not
make it any less worthy
of love. Your father made
you believe otherwise.
He made you believe
you needed to be without
fault in order to be loved.
But he was wrong.
Should you need any
proof of the matter,
then look just here."
—DAPHNE BRIDGERTON

KEY ENCOUNTER:
Daphne delivers her
speech about love and
perfection as the rain
falls on her and Simon.

WILL HUGHES-JONES ON BUILDING A BALL FROM THE GROUND UP:

We shot this long ball scene in February, so it's not warm outside. Daphne is wearing a very small, lightweight dress, and I knew it would begin to rain. We didn't want her to die of exposure or pass out; nor did we want to see everyone's breath in the cold. So we decided to do it inside and build a set that was just over twenty-five meters high. If you recall, it rains at the end of this ball! So we built a rain rig over the top of the set inside the studio. The whole set essentially stood in a tank that we constructed to hold the water. And then we heated the water to 34 degrees Celsius so that people could stand in the rain without getting cold.

We brought in all of the hedges and flowers, and then we handed the set over to a florist. And they did them in white, which was the wrong color. Eeks! Privately, I went to the head greensman and asked him if there was any way that they could change them to match the palette of the dresses. He redipped all of the flowers into a lovely dusky blue. It was a huge ask, but it completely transported the space. It was my favorite ball.

"The ball that I remember the most distinctly is the very last one, when Colin comes over to Penelope: The song that was playing on set was 'Crown' by Stormzy—it was such an intense moment for her, I'll never not equate it with that song."

—Nicola Coughlan

JACK MURPHY:

Stormzy is a British rap artist, and we danced to his song "Crown" at the Hastings Ball, which, fittingly, was the last thing we filmed. We had twenty-four dancers who could have broken out at any given moment to this song, and yet they were fantastically restrained and beautifully graceful, even though you could feel the energy bubbling beneath the surface.

I must admit, during that final dance between Simon and Daphne, I burst out crying. They danced so beautifully—and then it rains. I knew it was going to rain—it was in the script, after all—and I knew the final music would be the Max Richter piece, which has such a wonderful bounce to it. I wanted them to be like raindrops as they did a gallopade. And that's how I got them to realize and add to what is a very moving moment.

GOLDA ON PHOEBE'S PERFORMANCE:

At the Hastings Ball, when the sky parts and the rain pours down, we all stood around the monitor and watched this girl deliver this monologue in the most extraordinary, beautiful way. We were all so moved. Phoebe was just incredible. It was one of the last days of filming, and to see this actress deliver this monologue, having spent the last seven months creating this character, was the most beautiful finale you've ever experienced.

She's an extraordinary actress. And that moment for me was incredible. It was so joyous. I was so proud.

Hair & Makeup

The production theme of *Bridgerton* is marrying a respect for traditional Regency with a subtext—a subtle and sly wink of modernity. The wonderful late Marc Pilcher established the sensibility of the show. He had a lot of respect for the look and feel of the period, and he did a brilliant job of embracing this slyness in Season 1, which Erika Ökvist continued to grow and expand upon in Season 2.

Before we started shooting the show, we had a lot of conversations about the wigs—almost everyone, for various reasons, is wigged. Not only because we needed to achieve this heightened effect, but also because it's a lot easier to plunk a wig on a head than to style somebody constantly. The character of the wigs became a gigantic part of the show, and we were able to be really conscious about how everyone's hair evolved.

So Daphne's hair, for example, takes the same journey as Daphne. At the beginning of the show, she is the good girl who does exactly what duty dictates—you know, the Olympian of the season—and her hair is *tight* and perfectly demure and ready for war. It's her armor. But if you watch closely, you see the shape of her hair progress as she encounters Simon and the world of personal pleasure: It becomes more relaxed and softer, and you see her with her hair down. And in Season 2, she is a wife and mother and no longer a debutante. Her hair is grown up and elegant.

I was probably most obsessed with Cressida Cowper's headpieces, which are almost as incredible as Queen Charlotte's. She's pretty despicable. Her hair always matches the sentiment. It's very Medusa. I love how Marc made that sentiment literal. I also thought it was brilliant that when she's attempting to land Prince Friedrich, her braids are styled to resemble a crown— either to trick him into perceiving her as the perfect princess, or a presumption that she already has the job. And then I love that it evolves in Season 2 and softens *ever* so slightly. Like her, her hair has been taken down a notch or two.

We spent a lot of time on the Featheringtons, talking about their hair color. We wanted them to be a little bit gauche without turning them into cartoons—this would have been a challenge in less talented hands. We didn't want to push it too far so that people didn't feel they could relate to the characters: Marc and his team were always finding the balance between the fun and also ensuring that everyone looked their best.

Another example of character evolution through hair is Anthony—in Season 2, those wonderful sideburns are gone because he is no longer a rake. He's put his childish ways

behind him and is assuming the mantle of being a good son.

We loved Eloise's mullet in Season 1, and Erika Ökvist moved it forward—which seemed radical the first time we saw it—by giving her bangs. Now, bangs existed in the period, though they would have been styled slightly differently, but Erika added this big swash of modern hair that made us immediately able to identify with Eloise and her plight as she enters the marriage mart. We marked the transition with her hair while still keeping her Eloise.

Penelope's hair is slightly different in Season 2 as well. She's not hiding so much behind her hair, and it's a bit softer in places because we know her secret. Ultimately, as the characters grow and change, their hair changes with them.

Queen Charlotte's Wigs As Characters

TOM VERICA ON GOLDA'S WIGS—
AND THE GRIPS WHO SAVED HER BACK:

We had a lot of full-day scenes with Golda where she was in one of her incredibly heavy wigs. She would rehearse without her wig, because they're so heavy. Once it's on and we're shooting, we can't take it off. So I went to the grip department and asked if they could devise a contraption for her where she could basically sit down and have the pressure and weight taken off her head. They built her this incredible brace. Between takes or scenes, she can sit down and slide into a rig that releases all the weight off her spine. It's really a miraculous contraption. I'm so sorry we didn't think of that sooner!

SEASON 2 HAIR AND MAKEUP HEAD ERIKA ÖKVIST ON QUEEN CHARLOTTE'S WIGS:

We used the twist-and-tuck technique that is commonly used on textured hair, and then we built it up from there to reflect Georgian hairstyles of her time. Often executed in a swirl pattern or in straight cornrows braided from front to back, the shape of her braids was dependent on where the security needed to be for her wigs to stay in place and be balanced and comfortable. The weight distribution was always on our minds at this point because the weight of the hair can make the structure collapse. So we have to think about it the same way one would think about architecture. If we wanted to do a wig that shot straight up, we'd have to do crosshatching to accommodate for the crossweight, so it doesn't fall down. It's akin to the way you build a bridge with keystones.

HARRIET CAINS ON PHILIPPA'S HAIR:

Because my hairline is so low, I had to dye the bottom half and all the baby hair on my neck to match my wigs. So throughout the pandemic, my hair was loads of different colors, including ginger. I also had a short fringe during Season 1, which was glued to my head. I'd take that wig off and look an absolute state every single day.

Marc Pilcher looked after me—he could make magic with his hands. He'd just throw it on and make it perfect. Sometimes I would cry, just looking at his incredible work.

JESSICA MADSEN ON CRESSIDA COWPER'S HAIR:

When I first got the job, I envisioned it to be a very normal Regency production, like *Pride and Prejudice*. And then I tried on my costumes and had my hair done and was like, "Woah, this is *intense*." Marc Pilcher came in with a hairpiece with bows and pink strands, it was so extra, I loved it. He told me, "We've got to make it strong. I want it to be snaky. I want it to be solid, like a shield." Cressida's first season, she is really out there: Her hair is huge—it's almost threatening. In the second season, she has softened and come down from her pedestal slightly. It's still pretty big, but there are more flowers in there. And while her hair is pulled back and tight, it's not quite as severe.

SEASON 2 HAIR AND MAKEUP HEAD ERIKA ÖKVIST ON KATE SHARMA:

Kate is one of those people who looks amazing without any type of makeup. We're able to take a natural look and push it as far as we possibly could. Kate is also a no-nonsense character who doesn't feel that she has to have a new look every time she gets a new dress. We base a lot of her looks around her braid, whether it's worn down or up. We also wanted to connect back to her Indian heritage. When thinking about the riding scene, we imagined that she didn't want to wait for her maid to wake up to do her hair, as other ladies would—she simply braided it herself!

"There was a lot of up-front work, between teaching actors how to move, duel, box, and sing opera. And then, of course, there was the diction and bringing them all into the same world—we also had to work with Kathryn on her French accent, and Sabrina needed to sing in multiple languages. I put them all into physical training to get them into great shape—I eventually pulled Regé out of training because he was getting so big. I made them all come and do drop-in dance sessions and dance with the movement director, Jack Murphy. Polly Walker thought I was mad, but it brought me back to my early days doing theater. It was really such good fun."

—Sarada McDermott

BEYOND THE PAGE

BETSY BEERS ON ACTOR PREP

Another reason we really wanted Julie Anne Robinson to direct the pilot and Episode Six of Season 1 is that her prep is *meticulous*. She does an incredible amount of storyboarding and rehearsing and generally preparing and knows what she's going to do before she gets on sets. She and Lizzy Talbot, our intimacy coordinator, and Jack Murphy, our movement director, worked closely before there was anything to shoot.

And those two put such an incredible amount of energy into their roles, to show us something that you typically don't see—sex in a period drama, for one, and then period dancing that feels modern. Jack and I had so many long conversations with how contemporary we could push it. He was delighted, naturally, because he had done so many shows where everything was very, very period. I've never seen anyone smile harder. But we stressed we didn't want it to be parochial, but instead the spirit of modern dancing in the Regency style.

Throughout rehearsals, I encouraged him: "Make it dirtier, make it dirtier. Go further on that . . ." until we finally hit that point where it was like, "Okay, that might be a little too *Dirty Dancing*." I think it's remarkable that he was able to create an entirely new style, which really culminates in the first episode of Season 1 in that amazing sequence in front of the lanterns and fireworks. That's an incredible scene. And he did it again in Season 2 with Anthony and Kate—their dance was electric.

JACK MURPHY: There are two reasons to dance: to have pleasure or to give pleasure. There's show dancing and then there's social dancing. Social dancing is what we see in *Bridgerton,* and so I had to be mindful that the dancers I presented to Julie Anne and Chris for selection could create the world of the bon ton. We knew we wanted everyone to be within the ages of eighteen to thirty-five so we could reflect Daphne's storyline as a debutante. When she was dancing, we wanted her to be among her peers. It's fundamental that the dancers were aware that they were working in the world of drama, not dance. Therefore, the action within the dance is paramount—indeed, the step comes last!

We were either looking for actors who could dance very well, or dancers who could act very well. Because it was Shondaland, Netflix, and Julia Quinn, everyone wanted to audition. I was looking for a core group of twenty-four, and I probably started with two hundred before whittling them down.

In addition, Chris, Sarada, and I held many workshops with the supporting artists—for example, we did one on etiquette. I taught reverence, how to sit, and how to walk. We were really looking for the right quality of movement to be realized by all who filmed.

JACK MURPHY ON THE IDEA OF MOVEMENT AS ACTION:

Our personalities are indicated by the shape of our bodies and the way we stand, sit, and walk. Our movements and their motivation stem from physical, emotional, and mental sources. Our minds and feelings are informed by physical experience. Thoughts trigger emotions and actions. We sense our body, and we are aware of its energy. The outline of the body is the shape of its inner contents. Movement starts with an impulse, and movement is the emanation of thought. I encourage actors to connect to the physicality of the thought so that we get a corporeal presence. The dances are actioned—just like the dialogue.

JACK MURPHY ON REHEARSING:

I bring the company of dancers into the world of the episode by introducing them to the circumstances that lie within the scene; then I teach the steps. The dancers' ability to learn, process, retain, and perform up to six dances per ball was nothing short of miraculous, and their skill is humbling. They are always on point!

I encourage my dancers to work in neutral colors, for the women to wear a practice skirt and no makeup, and for the men to leave their sneakers at home. It's best for them to work in something that's akin to what their character will be wearing so they get the sense that this lives outside of themselves.

The dancers didn't need to train with corsets on, because they're used to them, but I will tell you that the actors needed practice. Ruth Gemmell had to dance a jig in Season 2, and she had the foresight to rehearse in a corset because she hadn't worn one since drama school. She wanted to remind herself of the sensation, because it does limit what is doable. No actor wants to be captured on the day unprepared!

SIMONE ASHLEY ON DANCING:
I did a bit of musical theater training when I was eighteen and a lot of ballet when I was younger—not to say I'm a ballerina, but I know how to move and hold myself, and I'm quite athletic. But I had never done period before, and it was amazing to work with Jack Murphy. He really fed confidence into us. That dance I did with Anthony was one of my favorite moments in the season. I poured myself into it.

JACK MURPHY ON ANTHONY'S DANCING:
In Season 2 we finally get to see Anthony dance, and of course, Jonny Bailey is extraordinary. He is an artist, and he's also a great athlete—so how did he dance? Beautifully. He had also done his research and knew that a man of his position would have been taught to dance by the dancing master from a very young age.

"The chemistry between Jonny and Simone is electric. They absolutely ruined me in one of their dances because they were performing my choreography, and I made the piece from my own experiences. To see Simone and Jonny embody my work was an incredible experience—I didn't realize I had gone to such a dark place in myself to create it."

—Jack Murphy

"That final dance and final ball is torture for him because we all know, as humans, that once you work out that you are in love, you still have to figure out how to communicate it. I think in that final dancing scene, there is a version where they both could have said the wrong thing at the wrong time and Kate could have left."

—Jonathan Bailey

Anatomy of a Scene
3X BALLS—ONE LOCATION

"Because of our tightly packed schedule, we used a council building in Bristol to film three consecutive balls—the Bird Ball, the Mirror Ball, the Ingenue Ball—not a palace but an office building. In one scene, where Simon escorts Lady Danbury down a hall, we built a tunnel out of fabric and strands in the orange room, which we had used for the ball the day before. It was very much a head-scratcher, but a total coup from our location team. You would never know from the Bird Ball or Ingenue Ball that we were not in a grand country home."

—Will Hughes-Jones

MIRROR BALL

DIRECTOR:
Tom Verica

LOCATION:
Tapestry Room,
Leigh Court, Bristol

KEY SONG:
"Simon And Lady
Danbury"
By Kris Bowers

BEST LINE:
"We must look like
we are enjoying ourselves.
As difficult as that
may be . . ."
—DAPHNE BRIDGERTON

KEY ENCOUNTER:
Daphne and Simon
unleash on the dance
floor with palpable joy.

CAST: Principles, plus
71 supporting artists,
including: 12 dancers,
4 musicians, and
8 footmen.

CREW: Principles,
plus 2 art directors,
2 home economists,
12 set dressers/props,
2 3rd ADs, 5 crowd PAs,
2 choreographers,
7 camera operators,
3 grips, 14 electricians,
1 rigger, 20 costumers,
25 hair-and-makeup
artists, 6 sound engineers,
2 script supervisors,
3 medics

"I think Tom Verica and I should be in Guinness World Records: *We did four balls, three in one building, a fourth in another building, in just as many days, with only one day off. I don't think it's ever been done. I also have to hand it to the brilliant Thomas Bassett, the first assistant director, because, my word, can he run a floor."* —Jack Murphy

TOM VERICA ON BLOCKING OUT THE BALL:

Because I had seventeen characters in this scene, and one conversation needed to seamlessly move into the next conversation, I had to lay out exactly where these actors were going to stand and how we were going to move through it. It could be that we followed a waiter with a drink tray, or a character goes on the move. It gets very intricate.

TOM ON *THE* DANCE:

We didn't know what music or score we were ultimately going to use for the ball, but it's probably the dance where Simon and Daphne had the most fun. Simon does a spin, which was not rehearsed, but it was a moment when, as part of that courtship, they were falling in love.

I had a library of music to pick from, and so I chose a song by Plan B—it had so much energy. Everyone was having a great time. You even see Adjoa bouncing along on the side—probably not period, but we wanted to make the moment feel accessible and modern, like everyone was swept away with the emotion.

Everyone kicked into gear when they heard that song—and in post, we laid in a fun classical piece that felt a little edgier than what you might have heard in Regency England. But it still belonged to that world. I like to think that what they were listening to was their equivalent of a fun pop song, a song that they could lose themselves to just a little bit.

BIRD BALL

DIRECTOR:
Tom Verica

LOCATION:
Morning Room,
Leigh Court, Bristol

KEY SONG:
"Bad Guy" by Vitamin
String Quartet

BEST LINE:
"Is my general ready
for battle?"
—DAPHNE BRIDGERTON

KEY ENCOUNTER:
Daphne endures some
tedious dances, then
teaches Simon all
about fan language.

CAST: Principles, plus
113 supporting actors,
including: 8 footmen to
the prince, 6 musicians,
12 dancers, 4 queen's
ladies-in-waiting.

**NUMBER OF
MACAWS:** 8

CREW: Principles, plus
1 home economist,
5 props, 1 scenic artist,
1 3rd AD, 3 crowd PA's,
1 choreographer,
5 camera operators,
4 electricians, 2 grips,
2 riggers, 26 costumers,
33 hair-and-makeup
artists, 4 sound operators,
2 script supervisors,
2 medics, 1 dialect coach

TOM ON DIRECTING DAPHNE'S TRANSFORMATION:

This was a very cinematic and dramatic scene, as it marks a major shift for Daphne in her journey. We needed it to be a significant moment as she descends the staircase, as if she's coming down out of the clouds to play the game.

We played with many different speeds as she works the room with her sudden sexiness and sultriness and her use of the fan—and we played with the position of each character so that the audience could really mark how they were receiving her. It was a meta moment of the audience watching them as they watch her. She's on display—but Simon is her real target. So I positioned Simon quite close to her and then had the prince cross in front of him, as everyone is in a bit of a trance, so that you see him working to get her attention. It created a dynamic attention shift, as the prince kneels at the bottom of the stairs.

I talked each character through the scene so that we could draw through what they were feeling: lust, jealousy, admiration, love, and more. For Violet, she's embarrassed by the display that Daphne is putting on. Meanwhile, the queen is absolutely loving it, and Lady Danbury is frustrated with Simon. You see all of that. You'll also note that the Featheringtons are right there, particularly Penelope—not only so that she can record as Lady Whistledown, but you can also sense her confusion, that "What the hell?" She knows Daphne, and this is a different Daphne entirely. There is a perceptible transformation.

INGENUE BALL

DIRECTOR:
Tom Verica

LOCATION:
Great Hall,
Leigh Court,
Bristol

KEY SONG:
"Feeling Exceptional"
by Kris Bowers

BEST LINE: "Why settle
for a Duke, when you
can have a Prince?"
—LADY WHISTLEDOWN

KEY ENCOUNTER:
Daphne and that fan,
man.

CAST: Principles, plus
67 supporting artists
including: 4 musicians,
12 dancers, 3 queen's
ladies-in-waiting, and
2 Prince Friedrich aides-
du-camp.

CREW: Principles, plus
1 home economist,
3 props, 1 3rd AD,
3 crowd PA's, 1 floor
runner, 2 choreographers,
5 camera operators,
6 grips, 6 electrical,
4 grips, 3 riggers, 22
costumers, 25 hair-and-
makeup artists, 4 sound
technicians, 2 script
supervisors

JACK MURPHY ON CHOREOGRAPHING PHOEBE:

When Phoebe was coming down the stairs during rehearsals, she didn't feel comfortable. She came over to ask me a question, and I was incredibly conscious that Tom was only six feet away. It was about how she was physically going to pull this off.

I looked over at Tom, and his eyes said, "Yes, of course, do your thing." And I told her, "You're feeling self-conscious coming down the stairs because everybody is watching you. So you're playing the feeling, not the action. As you come down the stairs, you realize—and there's a transition—that you have got to get 'someone else' to feel uncomfortable. And you are going to manipulate the prince in order to do so. So stop targeting your feelings and play the action."

Tom looked at me and smiled and asked if everything was okay. I thought I was in trouble. And I said, "Don't shoot the messenger, don't shoot the messenger!" And he said, "No, it's fine, it's good." And it was a very exciting moment for me because in the hierarchy, as a man much lower down the ladder than Tom, I felt affirmed. He not only approved but encouraged me to go further with my work. And Phoebe played that action very well—it is a powerful scene.

PHOEBE DYNEVOR:

It's very generous that Jack Murphy said I was merely self-conscious. I wasn't just uncomfortable, I was having a full-blown panic attack! I had woken up feeling like a pile of poo. Just one of those unfortunate days that we all have where we're just not feeling good about ourselves. And then I had to do this scene where I'm walking down the stairs while everyone is staring at me—it was so hard to confront all of those eyes. You always need an intention in a scene, and I just didn't feel like I deserved to command the attention of the whole room. I felt far too imperfect. I had a real moment with Jack where he coached me to a place of empowerment, but that was a really hard scene to film—I wanted to run away!

KRIS BOWERS:

There's a track called "Feeling Exceptional" which is played when Daphne comes down the staircase at the Ingenue Ball. It's a long slow-motion scene where she's using her fan and the prince and Simon are both watching her—actually, everyone is watching her. It's a great moment for her, and I had three or four minutes to really play with and expand that theme—we did all these variations and brought it into the orchestra. As you listen, you might not immediately recognize it as their song, but it's there, much as that scene becomes a pivotal moment for them—Daphne taking control and Simon realizing he does not want to lose her.

JANE KAREN, DIALECT COACH:

My mandate as a diction coach is to ensure that everyone sounds like they belong to the same family and the same society. There are so many variations on the English accent, and we had cast members who represented many of them. Nicola Coughlan and the actor who played Nigel Berbrooke are both Irish. The Regency-era Bridgerton accent is essentially posh British done with an American script, and because it's a Shondaland production, it's also very fast and sharp. In most period dramas, the actors could eat a meal in real time—it's slooooow. Brits also tend to drop the end of words and trail off their sentences, whereas Americans pronounce everything. I needed to be sure that all these English actors were enunciating while also saying everything quickly. I was laser-focused on clarity.

When we first started prepping, we didn't yet have scripts, so I wrote some fake Lady Whistledown stories so that the Featheringtons could read them to each other as though they were in the drawing room. We worked on a bunch of different options for Shondaland so they could see them as a family. For Kathryn's French accent, we did a lot of variations for them to choose from: Is it perfect? Is it obviously wrong? Then it was my job to ensure that we stayed in the approved version of the accent the whole time.

I also work with the actors to keep the scenes believable, particularly for scenes where they are displaying a lot of emotion: Does this level of anger make them seem too brutish? Are they calm enough? How would this character lose their temper? Because this is Regency society, they are typically very polite and English—so when someone says something terrible to them, how do they react? This is *Bridgerton*, after all, and there are a lot of people throwing shade around, and the Brits are excellent at statements that are quite rude and cutting. So the actors and I focus on how to get that just right.

SABRINA ON TRAINING TO SING ON THE OPERA HOUSE STAGE:

At that period in time, the arts were underrated; singers and actors weren't elevated like we are today. Siena very much had to rely on a man to clothe and feed her so she could continue to develop her talent. And what she does is hard. I had to fully commit to every single aria, and I did five months of preparation to be able to stand on that stage. I had to learn all the songs, including their pronunciation in different languages. First I had to get in shape, otherwise you don't have the necessary power. I worked with a coach on my French and my Italian. There were no shortcuts. There were days in the studio when I just needed to sit down and cry, it was so difficult.

It's funny because, initially, I auditioned for the role of Daphne. Then they called me in for Siena, who at the time was Italian, and so I worked with an acting coach and auditioned in Italian. I did three rounds for Daphne and three rounds for Siena. I knew Siena was an opera singer, but I didn't know much more than that. So when they cast me, they told me I'd be starting my training that week, and it was serious. I didn't know how much Rowan Pierce, a soprano from the San Francisco opera house, would be singing versus me, so we prepared as though I would need to carry all of it. It was wild, absolutely amazing.

I remember the first day I needed to sing in front of the cast and crew—it was sixty to a hundred people. And I was terrified. The execs were there as well. It was one of my first days on set, and I felt like I would be sick and pass out. The crowd was milling around, drinking their cups of tea, and nobody could hear the music except for me—it was in an earbud in my ear. And I started singing. And everyone stopped to look. I saw Phoebe, Nicola, and Jonny over in the car with their phones out, jumping up and down. They had heard me over the intercom and rushed upstairs to watch. As I finished, there was a pause, and then everyone started singing and clapping. I was crying. It was the most special day of my life, the way everyone showed up to support me. It was a magical experience.

JONATHAN AND THE LUKES ON FENCING:

JONATHAN BAILEY: The brothers get irrationally excited about the prospect of doing a scene that's just the three of us. At one point, we were being fitted for rowing outfits, and the production coordinator called to say, "We're thinking of setting you up with a rowing instructor," so we tried to sleuth it out. But while we originally thought we were going to be on the river, a few weeks later, we were learning how to fence.

LUKE NEWTON: We trained separately because of the COVID rules at the time—we couldn't rehearse together. And then we were finally allowed to come together and go through the routines. It actually made it quite fresh and kept us on our toes.

JONATHAN: We came up with the routines ourselves, and it was a true test of personality. Luke Newton is very patient and happy.

Luke Thompson is very steady, calm, and precise. And I'm a hothead, saying things like, "Yes, I mean I can understand what you're saying, but actually, I just think we should do . . ." So that was very exciting.

LUKE THOMPSON: No amount of training can prepare you for the very, very wet grass and the very slippery shoes. You feel very sensible, surrounded by a film crew in their civilian clothing while you're wearing floppy shirts and wielding swords. You really feel great and not at all ridiculous! But then to fall as well, in your tight, tight trousers and glorious waistcoat, is a real twist!

JONATHAN: I actually split the crotch of my trousers because I was halfway doing the splits. I managed to split my pants in Season 1 with Siena, too, so happy to stay on theme!

"Bill Richmond—on whom Will Mondrich is based—was a celebrity boxer at the time. He was born into slavery in New York, though he lived in the UK for most of his life."

—Dr. Hannah Greig

THE DENT SISTERS, HORSEBACK RIDING:

SAM DENT, HORSE MASTER: The most important thing we try to teach you first is your control and your confidence. Because once you have confidence on a horse and you feel like you're in control, everything else comes easy. Regé's character is quite cocky, so he needed to look like he really knows what he's doing. The first shot we have with him riding, we can't really double him because we pan around onto his face. So he has to be good by the time we do it. There's no choice.

REGÉ: Coming back in one piece is your first priority; looking good is maybe your second. You learn a physical language on a horse. You learn how you communicate with the horse a bit like how you communicate with a castmate. No offense to my castmates! It's a bit like getting on set with a more veteran actor who actually knows what's going on a lot more than you. And so you kind of have to pay your respects a little bit and go, "Look, I know that I'm new at this. I know you're better, but also, can I drive? Do you mind?"

CHARLOTTE DENT: Phoebe started off a little bit nervous, which was understandable. In most period films, they're riding with a weapon in their hand, but in Phoebe's position as a Regency lady, we worked on her relaxing her loose hand on her thigh.

KATE: I really fell in love with horseback riding. We worked really hard to get good at riding on camera.

LIZZIE TALBOT ON THE ROLE OF INTIMACY COORDINATOR:

Actors need agency, and they need to have a say in how they perform. So on some level, I'm there to be an advocate for the actors to ensure that they are always comfortable, but I am also helping them choreograph all the action so that they know precisely where to put their hands, mouths, and bodies. Once that muscle memory is locked, they can lose themselves a bit in the acting.

We have lengthy discussions about what the actors think each scene should look like. Then we go through various stages of choreography to see what works and what doesn't, and we create options for the director and cinematographer so that we can all arrive at a master plan together.

Bridgerton was unusual in that we were allowed a lot of rehearsal time, so we could try many, many, many different things as we worked it out. This is so much better than rushing to shoot; we'd already had the freedom to explore. Putting together intimacy that feels real and powerful is much more complex than jamming genitals together and rubbing up and down.

I think people are starting to recognize that intimacy is about so much more than fooling people into thinking you're having sex. Really harnessing that intimacy not only elevates the experience for the viewer but also empowers the actors. They don't want to feel objectified and self-conscious; they want to feel like they own their bodies and that they are not being gratuitous but are driving narrative and expressing the character within these most private of moments.

PHOEBE DYNEVOR ON BEING INTIMATE ON CAMERA:

I've done intimacy scenes in my career where you have no idea what's going to happen. The director calls, "Action" and tells you to "make it look passionate"—the other actor could do anything in that moment. It's a terribly uncomfortable position to be in, one where you don't feel safe in a moment that is already excruciatingly vulnerable. So to have an intimacy coordinator like Lizzy Talbot on *Bridgerton* was a game changer. We worked with Lizzy so closely: She coached us, we plotted out every single movement together—where you're going to put your hands and when, where you're going to move your body and when. This allowed the choreography to get into our bones. And because the boundaries are all established, it frees you up in loads of other ways, mainly that you feel safe and protected.

Those scenes look effortless, but they are really difficult to shoot—so nuanced and specific. Many took all day. Literally, Regé and I would be in a robe and slippers from eight a.m. to six p.m. When we finished the intimacy, we were elated—high-fiving and cheering that we got through it. It was so empowering to film those scenes and not feel like I was being gratuitously exposed, that they were part of my journey as I took control of my sexuality. And you'll notice that Regé was protective—because it was shot through the female gaze, you see much more of his body than you do of mine.

JULIE ANNE ROBINSON ON THE ROOM MONITORS:

In these country houses, there is no flexibility: You can't move the bed, you can't move the painting, you can't move the wardrobe. You have to be delicate with the furniture. In the duke's bedroom, which was in Castle Howard, Simon and Daphne spent a lot of time in that bed. There were room monitors who wouldn't leave. The idea of a closed set is absolutely sacrosanct, but for these room monitors, their jobs were more sacrosanct. They were in the scenes with us. We would be shooting, and they would say, "Can you go easy on the bed, go easy on the bedpost."

Sex Education in Regency England

"*Well, there are some things you ought to know. Some things that will happen that involve you and your husband. The duke, obviously. Well, he, you see, the marital act, which, now that you are married, you may perform.*"

–Violet Bridgerton

SHONDA: Oh, Violet—that marital-night pep talk was delightful. Though to be fair, sex education today is almost as feeble. I will say that I'm certain Violet's mother didn't sit her down and tell her what to expect—I give her credit for doing her best, with her own daughter, at a moment in time when there was just no script. That had to be so uncomfortable. And I also give her credit for not making it sound awful or shameful, or suggesting that sex is just for procreation. You can tell that Violet understands pleasure!

BETSY: Right. At no moment did Violet make her pep talk about pleasing Simon or go on about the duty of a wife to a husband—I can get down with rain and flowers and basset hounds. I do think it's very relatable today that Daphne would go into her wedding night and not have the information. You can expand this to modern times, if you think about the whole experience of being a woman. I don't have kids, but I would hear from friends all the time that nobody told them what to expect with childbirth or, really, with any stage of life. I think there's a general feeling, anyway, that we don't actually have all the information that we need when we go into a situation.

SHONDA: You know, to be fair, Daphne does find delight on the other side—and maybe there's an argument to be made that absent a firm idea of how it's supposed to be, it allowed her to let the experience unfold. It's a tough call, though: I would certainly want the tactical information! And she clearly feels enraged at her mother for making her feel so stupid and ill-informed.

BETSY: In Violet's defense, I think it also just speaks to how policed these high-society girls were, because as we know from that orgy scene, and Siena and Anthony's relationship, and Simon's rakish inclinations, and Marina's love affair, and from historical documents and caricatures from the time, everyone else was getting it on—all the time. It was a highly sexual culture. Except for women of a particular class. And not only were these women shielded from the act—or from touch at all—but they were also shielded from the information. And so we definitely can't pin the dearth of Daphne's education solely on Violet. Plus, does any child really want to learn about sex from their parents?

SHONDA: You have to applaud Violet's genius in coming up with the puppy story knowing just how little language she would have had around sex. But to answer your question? I think that's an unequivocal no. I also think everyone's collective hats are off to Simon for teaching Daphne how to masturbate, and so intensively prioritizing her own pleasure later. That was very important to all of us—not only that we capture the show from the perspective of the female gaze, but that it would be more about Daphne's desire, appetite, and delight than his.

BETSY: And she certainly had that—it's pretty revolutionary TV, even for today's standards, which is a damn shame. We all need to see more examples of women empowered in their sexuality—hats off to Daphne for paving the way.

DR. HANNAH GREIG ON SEX EDUCATION IN REGENCY ENGLAND:

We know from diaries from the period that women knew how to manage their bodies: They understood menstruation and, to some extent, pregnancy—not so much in specific scientific terms but that it required sex and took nine to ten months and so forth. There is absolutely nothing on sex education, which tells you everything you need to know.

VISUALIZING THE WORLD

WILL HUGHES-JONES ON THE LEGACY OF DIRECTOR DECISIONS:

Typically, pilot directors show up with all sorts of amazing ideas to really set the show, but as the designer, you have to be somewhat of a gatekeeper to make sure these ideas don't come and shoot you in the foot. You can really get into trouble halfway through the show when another director comes in and you're left with an idea that the pilot director came up with that doesn't work for the third director.

JULIE ANNE ROBINSON:

George Clooney has said that being a director is like being pecked to death by a flock of chickens. So much of directing is decision-making, or at least being able to figure out how to come to a collaborative conclusion. You have to be moving things forward all the time in order to keep pace with this type of storytelling.

Making *Bridgerton* was an incredibly collaborative process. Before shooting, we were on with the team in the U.S. all the time, going through decisions. For example, they asked me, "How many footmen do you want on the carriage, and what colors should their liveries be?" I'd never done a period drama, so I had no idea how many footmen went on carriages. So they told me to choose between four and six. I told them I'd take six. I wanted the highest number possible for every decision, so I also wanted six horses. Choosing the color of the livery also dictated the color of the carriage, which would dictate the wardrobe of all the servants. When you think about these old houses, they contained hundreds of servants, who would all be wearing the same livery. So even these tiny decisions had massive ramifications.

Director's Cut: Julie Anne Robinson
on Directing the Riding Scene

In Episode One of Season 1, Phoebe and Jonathan are on horseback, having a very long and important conversation—it is one of my favorite scenes that I've ever directed. For one, Phoebe needed riding lessons, but then in practicality, getting two horses to stay next to each other so I could get a nice two-shot or a single was impossible. It was horrific. At the end of the day, a crew member approached and told me that on every other period production in England, they use a mechanical contraption—two fake horses that bop up and down that you shoot against a green screen. So we have a scene that is actually very rare, two horses riding along. The actors did a brilliant job, though I apologized to them after for putting them through it. After all, the horses were really touchy, and every time you yelled, "Action," they would take off!

Anatomy of a Scene
THE LIBRARY

DIRECTOR: JULIE ANNE ROBINSON • EPISODE: 106—"SWISH"

SHONDA ON SNOWSUITS, SEXUAL INTIMACY, AND CREATING A SAFE SET:

Snowsuit, definition: weather-repellent outerwear worn by toddlers

On every production, I've always put out a memo to the actors to say, "If you want to wear a snowsuit while you're doing a love scene, then you will wear a snowsuit, and it's up to the director to figure out how to make that work." I've always been adamant about ensuring that every actor feels comfortable. But *Bridgerton* is basically about sex, which makes the idea of wearing a snowsuit impossible.

We have an intimacy coordinator on all of our shows, but having the right one on *Bridgerton* was vital: Without her, we would not have been able to get these essential scenes right. They needed to be as exciting for the audience as possible, while also preserving the dignity and the comfort of the actors. Lizzy really enabled us to create magic—it feels very real.

It's astonishing to me that there's been resistance to intimacy coordinators in the industry and that everyone is not embracing this role on set. You are not giving up any control, you are simply promoting a sense that these scenes are highly collaborative and that everyone will need to work together and build trust to tell a story that feels right. In *Bridgerton*, the sex is the narrative; we had to literally nail it!

JULIE ANNE ROBINSON: After the pilot, the producers asked me to do Episode Six for a pretty practical reason: The costumes were so elaborate and complicated and beautiful that shooting Episode Two immediately was unrealistic because of the number of balls. Episode Six—the honeymoon episode—involves very few clothes, and so it gave the costume department a chance to catch up. I told Betsy that would be fine. And then I read it and thought, "Oh my goodness! What have I just said yes to?"

But if Betsy asks me to do something, I usually do it. She's fantastic, one of the best producers I've ever worked with. And it was an interesting challenge, because it's tricky: We made an episode about something we can never see and speak of. Communicating that story without seeing it or speaking it is very difficult.

The scene on the ladder was the very first scene in the entire series that we shot. You don't have as many choices as you might think from the outset. This was at the Reform Club in London, which we had for one day, one day only. If you think about it, you have to spend a long time getting a large number of people dressed and ready. For the scene with Regé and Jonathan talking in their club and smoking cigars and drinking, there were a lot of background actors there. So we couldn't shoot that first. The other scene for the Reform Club was the intimacy scene in the duke's library. So we started there. That's how so many decisions in production ultimately are made.

It was just the two of them, and so we could do it first and make the most use of the day and the location. Phoebe and Regé are amazing troupers and said, "Hey, we may as well get used to this." And so off we went. I had already planned out the montage, so I knew what I was attempting. I hadn't storyboarded it, but I knew what I was going to do with it, and I had mapped out the other locations. So we went for it, because it was our only opportunity to shoot in that glorious space.

LIZZY TALBOT ON PHOEBE DYNEVOR'S VERY FIRST SCENE:

The Reform Club was men-only until the 1980s, so it was really fun to do a scene of female sexual pleasure in a space where women had only recently been allowed access. There was something really cheeky about that.

It was also the very first scene that Phoebe shot on *Bridgerton*, and Regé had only done a few others, so we threw them right into the intimacy fire. Of course, we needed to start with an oral sex scene on a library ladder—talk about reaching new heights! I asked them if they were ready to go, and they turned and gave me a quick thumbs-up and then burst out laughing—their first day of filming, and they were set to have oral sex on a ladder in a gentlemen's club.

TOM VERICA ON
THE IMPORTANCE OF PACE:

Shondaland shows have a certain pace, which is a constant reminder to the actors. There's only so much you can do in post, because it really comes down to cadence. Polly Walker, for example, was saying how refreshing the *Bridgerton* pace is because they've been trained to a certain cadence with period dialogue. They're taught to really make a lot of the words, versus the *Bridgerton* way, which is moving through the dialogue quickly. I needed to push the actors out of their comfort zone and really drive the pace. I used this metaphor in *Scandal,* but it holds for *Bridgerton:* You want to feel like you're in a car up on two wheels and that you could tilt the other way or fall straight down. If the actor has no idea where it's going, then that is exactly where we need them to be.

From a technical standpoint, you don't want the audience to see what's coming next. That's the energy that makes you feel like you went through the whole thing like a shot when the show ends. That's what we're going for.

The script supervisor gets a kick out of me because I'm always asking for the length of the cut—normally, a page of dialogue is a minute of screentime. I want that around forty seconds or low fifties. Not every scene is treated in the same way. We really want to *earn* the moments when there is nothing said and something is slow. We move, move, move, so that when we take a minute, it's important. Chris, Shonda, and I will know the minutes when we need to sit and enjoy; we plan for this. Those are the moments like Regé and the spoon, or the intimate moment in the gallery.

There is always a rhythm. When does the turn happen? How do we come in, and how does it end up? There's banter at the front of the scene. We really sat with the looks and hands barely touching. Those are designed elements to allow the intimacy of the moment that we've all earned through the courtship.

"Daphne watching Simon eat ice cream is an awakening for her—it's a moment where her attraction to him blossoms, and she's not quite sure what it is. We really wanted to slow it down to capture the way in which she is entranced by watching him eat, so we put it at a slower speed to put the viewer in her mind: You are watching her, watching him. And it is such an intimate moment in a very public place, where everyone is watching them, even as they pretend not to.

"We did that shot a bit tighter on Simon so that it almost had the feeling that she was kissing him or thinking about kissing him. We shot the rest of the scene in a traditional way except for that moment, which we really wanted to stress."

—Tom Verica

Anatomy of a Scene
THE PAINTING

DIRECTOR: TOM VERICA • EPISODE: 103—"ART OF THE SWOON"

TOM VERICA ON THE MOMENT THEY KNOW IT'S REAL:

One of my favorite scenes to direct was in the third episode when Daphne and Simon are in the side gallery and they first touch, skin to skin. It's a three-page scene with a big silent part that was written specifically to address that moment of connection. I find that incredibly seductive without being overtly obvious. In a lot of filmmaking today, people jump right into bed with each other. But in Daphne and Simon's "courtship," we were after the palpable chemistry and connection that they have, even if they're restricted from expressing it by Regency standards . . . and are still pretending that their flirtation is really just a ruse.

The DNA of the scene is that Daphne comes in as Simon is looking at his mother's favorite painting. Simon sees it in his own way; Daphne brings her insight. I had them face different directions because they clearly wanted to be near each other—but how do they bridge that moment? I really wanted the viewer to earn when they do finally look at one another, the moment where they take each other in.

I found it very sexy that there was the inevitable physical attraction, but we hold that off by keeping them metaphorically and physically looking in different directions, giving each other the side eye as they talk. I really wanted to earn when they do finally look at one another, the moment where they take each other in.

When Daphne finally turns, they start to come together, and you see them side by side. We did a very specific shot of just focusing on their hands as they feel the heat from each other. If you were to look at them from afar, you'd think that there were just two people looking at a painting and talking about it, but there was so much with the chemistry that Simon and Daphne brought to that—the tantalizing teasing and holding off. There was so much buildup to that moment where they finally have such a small, subtle, electrifying touch.

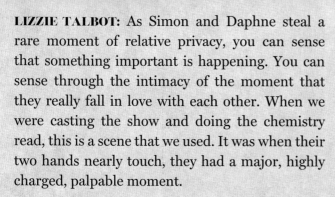

LIZZIE TALBOT: As Simon and Daphne steal a rare moment of relative privacy, you can sense that something important is happening. You can sense through the intimacy of the moment that they really fall in love with each other. When we were casting the show and doing the chemistry read, this is a scene that we used. It was when their two hands nearly touch, they had a major, highly charged, palpable moment.

PHOEBE DYNEVOR ON DAPHNE'S CHANGING PERCEPTION OF LOVE:

Daphne is young: She's eighteen, she's never been in love—she doesn't even know what that means. I think Simon realizes that he's in love with her before she realizes she's in love with him—and the scene in front of the painting really marks that for him. I think her attraction to him is immediate, but she doesn't let herself get carried away. We all have a romanticized version of love, and for young women, I definitely think there's an instinct to nurture and be motherly—it's in our heads. And Daphne is no different: She thinks she can save this man. Thankfully, she can, but it doesn't always end up that way.

TOM VERICA ON LIGHTING THROUGH TIME:

In terms of the craft of technical show making, I'm most proud of the work the team did on the scene when Lady Danbury brings twelve-year-old Simon to confront his father. Initially, Simon doesn't stutter—and you can see a hopeful expression pass across his father's face that maybe his son is the duke he wanted after all—before Simon gets nervous and his speech breaks down again. His father essentially shuts the door on him.

In the next scene, current-day Simon is in the same room, and he's sitting in the father's chair, playing back this memory. It would have worked beautifully if you just cut to Simon sitting there, but I wanted to create a connection to the despair in young Simon as he turns from his father. So I put young Simon and current-day Simon in the same shot. The camera pans instead, and midway in the same shot, the lighting crew transitions the scene from day to night. We made a dividing line in the room that marked the transition. The guy who was cueing really had to nail the timing. That was a major technical achievement that involved almost every department. Regé loved that moment, too, because it gave him a chance to really connect with the pain of his younger self at this final encounter with his father.

CHERYL DUNYE ON THE DELIGHT OF CINEMATOGRAPHER JEFF JUR:

Jeff Jur, the cinematographer, created the whole look of the show. And you think someone of Jeff Jur's caliber would be tired and be like, "Girl, I'm out." But he is the most gentle guy and would want to meet on the weekends to talk about what we were going to shoot. We were both like kids. He stands at the wheels—where you stand to work the cameras—whereas a lot of directors of photography sit down and direct the team. Jeff worked the whole time. He was on set way before me, and I was tired, but he had endless energy. He was always wanting to meet, and talk, and come up with the blocking, and be sure that I was getting all the shots I wanted and needed. He is just a wonderful guy. On his cart, where he stood and manned the wheels, he also had a little Nespresso machine. And he would always be making and offering me espressos. He was taking care of me 200 percent, anticipating all of my needs.

DIRECTOR CHERYL DUNYE ON SEASON 2'S BIG SEX SCENE:

This was not an easy scene. Chris Van Dusen really wanted this scene to be shot outside, under the moonlight, on the ground. And it was November! To get all of those clothes off romantically—she's wearing a corset!—and to make it look romantic is not easy. Jeff Jur and I had to figure out how to shoot around it, when to go wide and tight, what we could potentially shoot on the stage inside, and how to shoot the outdoors wide. We also had to figure out how to make it seem like they're hot, even though it was winter out, and one a.m., and freezing.

The other big conversation around this scene—which the viewers had been waiting for with so much anticipation—is that our Brown leading woman is going to have sex out of wedlock, whereas our white leading woman in Season 1 had to wait until she was married. I tossed those ideas to Chris and Tom Verica. They completely understood, and so the scene became entirely about her pleasure and Anthony giving to her.

SIMONE ASHLEY ON THE SEX SCENE:

Working with Cheryl was similar to how I worked with Jonny: We didn't have loads of conversations, it was quite unspoken. She just got it. And she paid a lot of attention to details, particularly in our intimacy scene. As she said, "This is an Indian girl we're seeing on-screen, maybe for the first time like this, and we want it to be empowering for her." And so we turned it into a better, even saucier moment, where we see Anthony giving pleasure to Kate. It's really important to portray women in their sexuality having power and confidence and getting what they deserve.

SHONDALAND EXEC ANNIE LAKS ON THE TIGHT SETS AND STAYING ON TIME:

My job on set as the Shondaland representative is to ensure that we're getting everything we need—all the options. This requires a lot of on-the-job problem-solving, as every day you'll have a host of new and interesting issues. It is completely unpredictable!

One Friday night near the end of filming Season 1, we were double baking, which means we were filming two episodes at the same time. It also meant that there were two directors and two completely different crews racing to finish work for the week on this Friday Night. As we were coming up to the end of the day, time was running out and we needed to get two critical scenes done—and, of course, they happened to be in the exact same location. In the octagonal set, we had Siena and Anthony going at it, per usual. And *just* down the hall, we had the scene where Lord Featherington dies. While the sets were in a massive warehouse, these two small and intimate sets were tight and close together—*and* we were shooting an intimacy scene in one, which meant that it was a closed set, and there were very few of us at the monitors. But many people needed to be near, including hair, makeup, costume, etc.

Because of sound constrictions in that tight space, we couldn't film both scenes concurrently, so we were switching back and forth and back and forth, and we were running out of minutes. I'll never forget standing in front of those monitors, with the eyes of hundreds of people on me, as we would yell, "GO FOR SEX! GO FOR DEATH!" over and over again. That was pretty much the show, captured in one Friday evening.

ANNIE LAKS ON GETTING EVERYONE PUMPED UP:

Jeff Jur, the cinematographer, knew exactly how to get everyone's energy up. We were filming the Featherington Ball in Season 2 and it was about three p.m. and everyone was flagging. So during a break, he just blasted *Saturday Night Fever* into the ballroom. Everyone started going nuts in their Regency costumes and had a dance break in the middle of the ball. It was really fun to see everyone cut loose.

Music was a big part of our life on set. And we loved a full-set dance party. Jack Murphy choreographed a dance for everyone to "We Are Family" for needed breaks. And when we wrapped Golda for Season 2, we played her off the set with "Dancing Queen"—the whole crew went crazy, dancing for Golda. So we started a tradition of playing everyone else off for the season with different songs.

Julia Quinn on the Pall Mall

The interaction of the characters in the pall-mall scene is so familiar to anyone who has a brother or a sister. I joke that the Bridgertons could have turned croquet into a blood sport: They are so snarky and competitive with each other, in a way that you can only be with your siblings. It's not so much that they care about winning, they just want each other to lose.

This is a fan favorite scene in the book, but it almost wasn't in there—I felt like the story was happening too rapidly, and I hadn't done a good job of showing that Kate and Anthony no longer hate each other. And so I started to wonder what the one thing could be to convince Kate that Anthony is not such a bad guy. And I decided it would be seeing him interact with his family, especially in a crazy, snarky way. Nobody can be a bad person who interacts with his family like that. They are ready to hit each other over the head, but there is real love there. It ended up being multiple chapters long because it was so fun to write.

When Netflix first released some photographs, they showed a shot of Simone Ashley holding a rifle with Anthony and Benedict and Jack Featherington in the background. She looked so fierce, it was amazing. But readers were flipping out, thinking Shondaland had replaced pall-mall with shooting.

Theoretically, it could have been any sport. But when I was a kid, we went to my grandparents' house all the time, and in my mind, they had an enormous backyard, probably because I lived in a little condo with no yard. Their next-door neighbor had a croquet set in the shed, and she told us we could go in there and play whenever we wanted. It was our favorite thing to do—we would put wickets over tree roots to make it really hard.

"We have a really talented writers' room: They do a great job of outlining the shape of the season and where it's going to finish. And then we execute against that as best we can. Something else might pop a bit more, like an actor's performance. Finally, there's the magic that Shonda brings in the third stage of writing, which is editing. She is never handcuffed to the script but will look at the board and move things around. She's a master at elevating the drama, the moments, and finishing that punch."

—Tom Verica

POST-PRODUCTION
THE FINAL STAGES OF STORYTELLING

Putting All the Pieces Together

"Normally, you would shoot with a director until they completed their episodes from start to finish. Then you would pass each episode on to the post-production team so they could start editing while you moved on to shoot the next episode. But instead, we were shooting half of an episode at a time and then going back to finish them at the end when we could finally access our rebuilt sets. It became the most complex puzzle of all of our careers."

—Sara Fischer

BETSY: The last time I saw Shonda in person before COVID was March 13, 2020—about two weeks after we finished shooting *Bridgerton*. Like the rest of the world, we shut down the office and assumed we'd be back together in a few days. As it turns out, we ended up editing the entire show over Zoom. Which, if I'm honest, did have its upsides—like easy access to snacks.

SHONDA: Hey, I edited the whole thing in my pajamas. Definite upside! But honestly, having cuts of the show to watch really got us through the pandemic—it made it ever so less dramatically horrible; it took the sting off. Because just when you thought it couldn't get any worse, you got to see an episode of *Bridgerton*.

BETSY: And the normalcy and routine of an editing process became a touchstone—we would get together and give notes and exchange experiences. It made it all feel a little less lonely and remote.

SHONDA: Working with the editors is one of our favorite times, too, because while it doesn't get all the glory, it's the final stage of storytelling. The show is first made when you write the thing, next when you shoot it. But the third time is when all those pieces come together and get scored and mixed.

BETSY: Working with the editors is also one of your many genius points. I remember when I first met you, and you had never edited a show before. And, if I'm honest, I was pretty good—I'd certainly been in some editing rooms in my time, I was pretty freaking cocky about my skills. So how pissed was I when, within ten minutes, you had figured out the best way to tell the story with no training?

SHONDA: Well, one of your genius points is music. You are a music guru, and you always know how to find the right tone through the right song. You can also put into words exactly what you want in a way that every composer can immediately understand. I think I have good taste in music, particularly when it comes to what we call needle-drops, which are the songs you hear playing in the back of big dramatic moments—but very often I don't have strong feelings at all and really have no clue. In those moments, I need you to take that ball and run it down the field. I thought what you and the team did with the music in *Bridgerton* was genius. That was something I wouldn't have done, and it worked beautifully.

BETSY: And in theory, it could have been a disaster. I remember saying to you, "What if we took songs people recognize and play them as though they're from the period?" I think it was so successful because through every point of production on *Bridgerton*, we wanted it to feel of the period but give enough modern elements so that anyone could relate to it. Bridging the music in this way felt like we weren't taking anyone out of the period, and we also weren't hitting them over the head with the time period.

Teamwork:
A Conversation with Post

SCOTT COLLINS, HEAD OF POST-PRODUCTION: *In any show, there's a fine line that we find in post between scope and story: You want those big, beautiful wide shots, but you also want to be tight and intimate and hear what's going on. So we're constantly shifting between scope and story.*

The stage directions are also critical—a lot of the show is in those small details that Shondaland is really known for. It's what the actors say, of course, but so much of the show happens between moments of dialogue. That's captured by the writers and put down on the page. We want to get the lines, but that first edit is also about all the things that aren't said.

GREG EVANS, EDITOR: *Before I begin editing, I watch absolutely everything—all the different options. As I go, I mark anything that I think is intriguing, that gives me a reaction. I also keep in mind that it always needs to be from the female perspective; it's easy to slip into what we typically see, which is focusing the gaze on the women. So, for the ball scenes I was doing, I was specifically looking for moments where the viewer would be thinking about kissing Regé, for example. The first cut matches the script. Even when I have a sense that something isn't working, I want the director I'm working with, the showrunner, Shonda, to all see it so we can have consensus that it's not right.*

And we're trying to keep it fast. One of the things we always talk about is that if you keep up the pace a majority of the time, when you do slow down, it's twice as effective.

HOLDEN CHANG, POST PRODUCER: *The shots and sets were so beautiful, you could linger. But by keeping it going, we kept it interesting. As we go, the shows get tighter and tighter.*

SCOTT: *It pays off, because when you need emotional tension, you add in long and uncomfortable beats, and the audience really feels them.*

GREG: *After I do my edit, the director will do their own cut. What's great about Shondaland shows is that Shonda and Betsy watch all the different versions—they want to see various perspectives and are open to everyone's point of view. Early on in my days at the company, Shonda said to me, "I don't want you to just tell me yes—if you don't have a POV, then you're not really helping." That's always been in the back of my mind, to bring something to enhance the overall vision.*

HOLDEN: *That's one of the distinctions in television: There are a lot of different voices and visions, including that of the showrunner. While we had four directors, Chris Van Dusen was our constant. Season 1 was his first year as a showrunner, and so Betsy was there for many of the early stages, and then she stood back and let him run on his own.*

SCOTT: *The directors deserve a lot of credit, particularly on the first season. All the episodes finished at the same time, which is intense. Not only is that tough on the editors, but it was hard on production to jump around in time and season, and neither our team nor the directors had continuity.*

GREG: *I left in the middle of my block to go and shoot another TV show! I cut all the location material—I had the duel, so that was a big dramatic moment—scored, and sound-designed it. And then I left for a couple of months because I needed the second half of my footage! That definitely never happens.*

SCOTT: *It ended up giving all the directors a lot of time with their footage. Normally, they're moving so fast they barely have time to watch scenes before they're on to the next, but because they each had a break, we gave them an early cut of all the location footage that was missing interiors—so they went into their time on set knowing how all the exteriors played.*

HOLDEN: *The wildest part is that we got through this production—which had gone wrong in so many fundamental ways, and yet the whole team continued to save the day—and then . . . COVID. One week after filming, we shut down the offices. Normally, we would do this all together.*

SCOTT: *Shondaland has a beautiful post-production facility, with all of these editing bays and areas for viewing footage together. And we couldn't use any of it.*

HOLDEN: *Typically, you hire a full orchestra for the score, and Kris Bowers would have been there live, conducting. It all went sideways.*

GREG: *Editors are inherently paranoid. We spend a lot of time in dark rooms! Holden had a year's supply of hand sanitizer, wipes, and most importantly, drives.*

HOLDEN: *A week or two before the shutdown, I sent a PA out on a shopping spree. I knew that if we didn't have hard drives and our central server was inaccessible to the editors, they couldn't work on the show. Ultimately, there was a run on hard drives just like there was on sanitizers, but we fortunately got there first!*

GREG: *Normally, we'd do reshoots just to make everything perfect and be sure we had options for every bit of connective tissue.*

HOLDEN: *We were supposed to shoot Daphne and Simon dancing on a cliff top—that was on the list—but we ended up shooting them dancing in a gazebo instead. The cliff would have been dramatic, but that dream sequence worked just fine.*

GREG: *There was nothing fundamental that we needed, particularly when it came to the overall identity, the things that carry over. In the first season, we define some elements, like how we do flashbacks, or sound elements like the Lady Whistledown theme, or how we're going to cut to keep the pace and energy going. After living in this world for a year, we definitely know how to approach those balls.*

SCOTT: *One of the biggest wins for future seasons is that Julie Andrews can now record her voice-overs at home, and so we have her in our temporary cuts going forward. For the first season, we hired a SAG actress to do the voice-over until we had a final locked script for Julie—we didn't want to bring her into a studio during the pandemic until we knew exactly what we needed. The only problem with this was that the pace of the actress was a lot quicker, and so when we went to place Julie Andrews, the timing was totally off.*

Speaking of sound, the sound mixers, Westwind, are incredible. We were able to give them five or six days per episode, whereas most shows wrap in under two days, so they had time to play in this world. They are pulling the music, dialogue, and sound effects into one visual identity: This is the sound of the carriages pulling up in front of the house, the horsemen, the tinkling of dishes and trays. They are elevating some sounds, adding others. It's actually pretty wild to consider what's required to make a world feel real and yet not distracting or overwhelming.

HOLDEN: *In addition to sound mixing, we worked with a colorist at Technicolor Hollywood, and then our VFX team, who are effectively Photoshopping the show, frame by frame, shot by shot. We shoot scenes that are supposed to span seconds or minutes over the course of four hours, so the VFX team needs to ensure that the lighting looks consistent. They also spent a lot of time making it look bright, sunny, and warm. We had to replace a lot of gray skies with bright blue ones. In some scenes we even had to paint out visible breath because it was so cold when we shot scenes that were meant to be summertime. Besides those scenes with rain, we were trying to create a perfect world.*

The Music That Made the Show

MUSIC SUPERVISOR ALEXANDRA PATSAVAS:
I'm always excited when there's a new Shondaland project because there's a new sound signature to uncover. (To date, I've worked on all their shows, beginning with the *Grey's Anatomy* pilot.) They sent me a script, which I felt like I could really understand musically, and so we met to talk about it before cameras started to roll. We really dug into what the score should be and how music could partner with the other creative teams. Obviously, the costumes and production design are full of Regency references, yet they also had permission to be modern, which is exactly what we wanted to achieve in sound. We focused on instrumentals first, though in all Shondaland shows, we do a big, rough ideating phase first, where

we throw around a lot of ideas and options. Chris Van Dusen is a big Max Richter fan, Betsy was really interested in instrumental covers, there's modern instrumental by Sufjan Stevens, we knew we wanted some pop, and so on. With that direction, I went and started to compile lots of tracks to listen to, including a lot of covers.

BETSY: I had this experience years ago with a group I love called Rodrigo y Gabriela. They're a Mexican group who were thrash metal musicians and couldn't get any work. So they started going to resorts and would play punk and rock-and-roll songs as though they were flamenco. So you'd be sitting in these really posh resorts, thinking you were listening to flamenco, but really, it's "Stairway to Heaven." I fell in love with this idea of stealth music. It seemed critical for *Brid-*

gerton. That the music would seem period, but somewhere in the back of your head, you're going, "I recognize that, I recognize that song."

ALEX: I pulled hundreds and hundreds of options, often as many as ten songs for one spot. They go "in the bins," so that they're available to the editors as they cut scenes and they place music to see what fits.

For a cover to be effective, especially an instrumental, the viewer really has to grok it. These pop songs had so much resonance and were so modern that it really worked—and it was seamless with the storytelling and with Kris's score. I remember watching some of the early cuts of the show that were just delicious—as a fan as well as its music supervisor. Toward the very first ball, when Daphne pulls up to the cover of Ariana Grande's "Thank You, Next," I was pretty thrilled. It set up our musical landscape, and it was a wink at the audience.

COMPOSER KRIS BOWERS ON NAILING THE PERIOD THROUGH SOUND:

When Scott Collins first called me about *Bridgerton*, I was very excited. I'm a pretty romantic guy—ask my wife—*and* I also love working with Betsy, Shonda, Scott, and Tom.

Scott told me a bit about the vision and that the music would need to rise to the grand level of the show as well. I really wanted to push myself—writing huge orchestral pieces is a rare opportunity. At first I thought I would write something specific to the era, as it was such a strong period for classical music in Europe—Mozart died in the 1790s, Beethoven was still composing. But it just didn't feel right for the show to go completely classical: It was too expected.

Next we went in the complete opposite direction and tried something incredibly modern, using orchestra music almost as samples. In one of the ball scenes, we had something like Kanye placed—very aggressive brass instruments, lots of synth sounds—and it was just wrong. It felt like the clash of two cultures rather than a bridge.

Ultimately, because I started writing the music while they were still shooting (music is generally scored in post-production), I had a lot of time in the sandbox to try different things. What unlocked the sound for me was Simon and Daphne's theme. Chris Van Dusen asked me to write that theme so they could shoot to it—Daphne plays part of it on the pianoforte. I sent him some Ravel and other impressionistic music to get a sense of what he wanted, as I knew it needed to be something in that world, because you can feel the romance in that style.

I say "impressionistic" because there's something recognizable about that style of painting. You can tell that there's a lake or a pond, but it's a little dreamy. That's the sensibility that I was going for with sound instead of brushstrokes. It's emotional, without giving *too* much feeling, because you want the scene to do most of the heavy lifting. But the music needs to support the theme—it can't be distracting, and it can't be overbearing. It has to be just right.

"In Daphne's piano scenes when she is playing her theme, the audio is of me, but Phoebe did actually learn how to play the piece—she worked with a teacher to be able to play it. That is impressive! It was a very difficult piece, which I realized when I went to record it—I had to rehearse a lot. The piano playing in the show is spot-on: Whenever you see shots of her hands, they are completely [right] in terms of which notes are being played."

—Kris Bowers

SCORING:

When I score a TV show or a movie, I do it at the end, in conjunction with the editors and other processes in post-production. The music supervisor will place some preexisting music, and then I compose the rest. Music is one of the last parts to come together because I score according to the cues of the editors. As they edit, they will place temporary music—something sourced from another film or a music library—and that allows them to create the pacing and the rhythm they're after. And I use that to score.

Typically, every single time something significant happens in the show, it will be on a big beat of music—or, occasionally, the opposite. Sometimes they'll displace the cuts ever so slightly intentionally. Regardless of direction, the way an editor uses the music dictates how I will write to that cue.

Before I began to write, I sat down with Chris Van Dusen and we did a spotting session, where we watched the show together and talked through what he wanted in various scenes along with his feelings about the temp music—whether it closely aligned with his vision or he wanted a different direction. If everyone loves the temp music, then it's up to me to parse why: Is it the pace? The instrumentation? Is it an aspect of the orchestration? I take those insights and then figure out how to approach the score, how to do my own thing.

Obviously, rhythm is a huge part of any score—sometimes you can simply match the tempo of the temp music; other times you'll just need to hit the cues of the editor. In the duel scene, for example, I changed the tempo from the temp music, but then switched the tempo again when we transitioned to Daphne pacing in her bedroom. I needed to do something really dramatic in that moment. That's a good piece of score to understand how there's an overall arc to a scene and then important punctuation moments where things shift—throughout, I'm trying to create the connective tissue between all of these.

I loved contemplating the balls. When you're first reading a script, you're never quite sure how big the scope should feel, which can really affect the musical score. If you want something that's intimate, you use fewer instruments, for example. But with *Bridgerton,* we were able to play with incredible scale because you have intimate moments between these characters, heightened love stories, and at the same time, grand balls and massive events in big houses and palaces and gardens. It gave us a lot of opportunities to do bright and huge orchestral pieces, which you rarely get to do on TV.

Chris Van Dusen really wanted the score to match the world, so if they were focused on a violinist in a band, he would want me to play up those tones, but other than that, we didn't use the interpretation of the band we're seeing as the basis for the instrumentation—it didn't need to be a perfect match. After all, most of the ensembles were pretty small, whereas we wanted the balls to feel really grand and full of sound. The score is much, much larger than what the band could create.

VITAMIN STRING QUARTET:

Alexandra Patsavas, the music supervisor on *Bridgerton* and so many other Shondaland shows, is a legend in the industry. She knows how to take the right angle with the music she picks for a show—and she picked a lot of Vitamin String Quartet pieces for the first season.

They are one of the best groups at covering pop songs in a classical way. They can hear an entire song and convey it with so much beautiful musicality. And at the same time, someone who isn't in the industry can listen to it and say, "Oh, I know that song." These are songs that can make the audience feel exactly what the characters feel.

HOW THE SOUNDTRACK CAME TOGETHER:

It will surprise listeners to know that none of the musicians were ever in the same room together. When it was time to create the music, we were deep into the pandemic, and so each musician recorded by themselves at their house—and they each layered themselves multiple times. So when you hear a huge string orchestra—like during the duel—that is actually only five or six musicians who have recorded themselves over and over again and pieced it all together.

After we finished, I felt such a huge level of gratitude for the musicians on this project. It's one thing to write something and not have a full sense of how it will sound but be able to bring a bunch of musicians into one room to play it together. That's an incredible experience, to be able to play with a band and bring something to life in an emotional and intentional way. But we were all alone, creating music together completely apart—and then we brought it all together, and it worked and was still resonant and powerful. I spoke to the flutist on the project, and she said that when she heard a cue for her to layer in her part, she felt emotional because somehow, we managed to make it feel like she was still playing with an orchestra, something that hadn't been possible for such a long time. It really speaks to what these musicians put into these recordings.

ESTABLISHING THE THEMES:

The thing I love about certain composers is their ability to take one small theme and be exhaustive with it: It subconsciously connects us to the story of that character. John Williams (*Jaws, Star Wars, Schindler's List, Raiders of the Lost Ark*) is a master of that. If you listen carefully in *Star Wars*, for example, you'll hear so many subtle references to Princess Leia's theme. It reminds you of Princess Leia without you even realizing it.

All of the moments between Daphne and Simon are centered around their theme, which is what Daphne plays on the pianoforte: It was so useful to create that in the beginning, so Daphne could play it. It became something I could refer to throughout the score. Every time you see them struggling with something, the music might feel emotionally different, but the theme is still tucked in there. As we go through all of their various climaxes as a couple, you feel additionally moved by it because you've heard the music shift and evolve alongside them. It is very subtle, but if you go back and watch the show, you'll notice that it's always there.

SHONDALAND EXEC ANNIE LAKS
ON SHOOTING PICKUPS:

It's very, very expensive to turn the cameras back on after you shoot, even though every production invariably does reshoots or needs to add things after the fact. Because of the pandemic, we had to work with what we had shot—thank God what we had was great, and naturally, we had created a lot of options. The only thing that we shot after the fact was the Lady Whistledown reveal. It was not originally in the script, but in the editing room, Shonda decided we needed to bring the viewer in on the secret, and she was absolutely right.

The Ending That Didn't Make the Cut

**ALISON EAKLE ON THE
NEW ENDING TO SEASON 1,
EPISODE ONE:**

Originally, Episode One of Season 1 ends on a little newspaper boy delivering *Lady Whistledown*s. Initially, the paper had been free to introduce her and get everyone hooked on wanting more juicy gossip. So it ends with the queen, who can't wait for *Whistledown,* and the little boy, who tells her that it'll be fivepence. And her line is "Pay the boy!" because she, too, is desperate for her hot goss. In the editing room, Chris and Shonda evolved the ending significantly, dropping that final moment where even the Queen pays for Whistledown, and instead ended on the moment at Vauxhall Gardens, where Daphne and Simon dance in front of the fireworks for the whole ton to see. And on top of that, they then had the idea to intercut *those* moments with the post-Nigel punch discussion where Simon designs the ruse he and Daphne will play out. Initially, that scene had just played out linearly, prior to them walking onto the dance floor. So, in this new version, you now have Simon hatching this plan, Daphne questioning if it will work, *all* intercut with actually seeing it unfold brilliantly. It was incredible, and so dramatic, a great example of how episodes would evolve with each stage of the process.

CONCLUSION

And so, Dearest Reader, here is hoping that you have delighted in this peek behind the scenes of *Bridgerton*.

As we all know, each child of the family gets their own season and happy ending. When they're not basking in their moment in the sun, they are part of the narrative fabric, the weaving of so many different stories and lives that give our world its color and texture. It's a wonderful metaphor for production, really: each person comes forward to do their part and then waits eagerly before being called on to enter again.

Our hope is that this book makes you more interested, invested, and curious about *Bridgerton*, of course, but also about world-building in general, and the exquisite care that goes into every moment of production, whether it happens onscreen or off. Just like in *Bridgerton*, production is its own dance: It's rhythm, pacing, and carefully choreographed steps that are lovingly orchestrated. It's the most intricate and over-the-top ball of them all. And we are delighted you chose to join the party!

—**Betsy Beers**

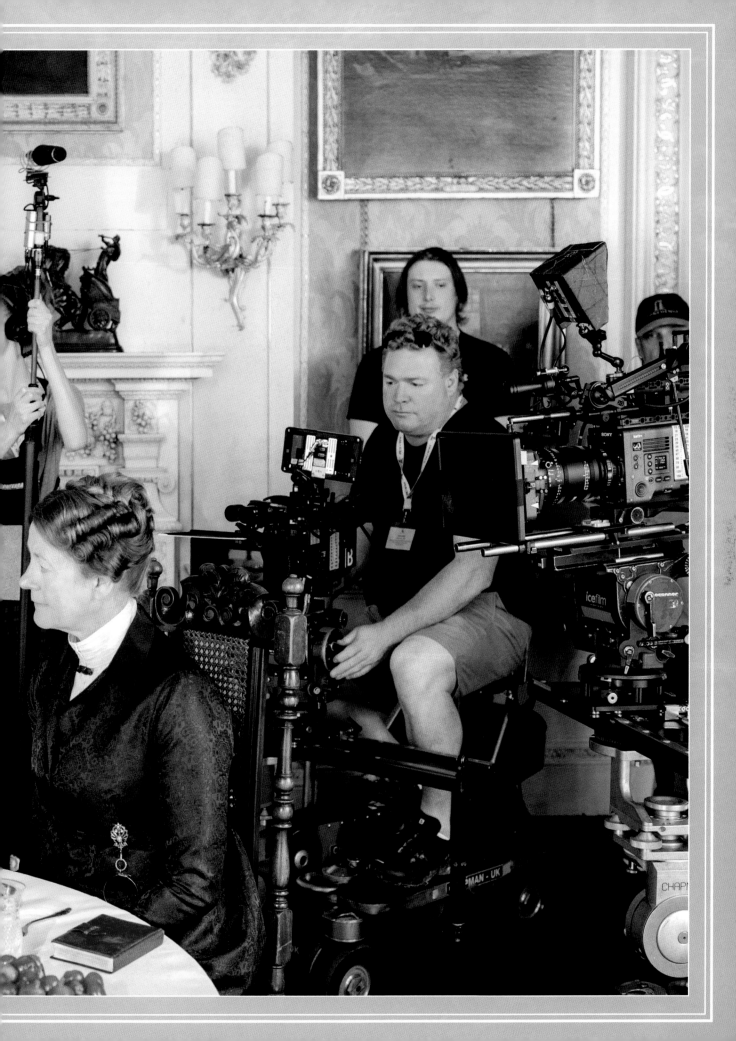

Cast

Adjoa Andoh

Al Nedjari

Amerjit Deu

Amy Beth Hayes

Anand Desai-Barochia

Andromeda Godfrey

Anthony Head

Anthony Wise

Ash Hunter

Ashley Campbell

Bailee Carroll

Bailey Patrick

Ben Miller

Ben Prout

Bert Seymour

Bessie Carter

Bill Ashbridge

Brig Bennett

Cairo Eusebe

Calam Lynch

Caleb Obediah

Caroline Quentin

Cate Debenham-Taylor

Celine Abrahams

Celine Buckens

Charithra Chandran

Choy-Ling Man

Chris Fulton

Claudia Jessie

Daphne Di Cinto

David Sterne

Dempsey Bovell

Dixie Newman

Dominic Coleman

Duncan Watkinson

Edward Cartwright

Edward Jones

Eleanor Nawal

Elle Meadows

Emilia Danks-Smith

Emily Barber

Emma Beattie

Emma Naomi

Esme Coy

Euan MacNaughton

Florence Hunt

Frances Pooley

Frank Blake

Freddie Stroma

Gabrielle Oke

George Kemp

George Watkins

George Wigzell

Georgia Burnell

Georgia Slowe

Geraldine Alexander

Gilly Tompkins

Golda Rosheuvel

Grace Stotesbury

Hamish MacDougall

Hannah Donelon

Harriet Cains

Helene Maksoud

Hugh Sachs

Huxley Sheppard

Ian Keir Attard

Jack Ward

James Bryan

James Fleet

James George

James Matthews

Jamie Beamish

Jarren Dalmeda

Jason Barnett

Jessica Madsen

Jessie Baek

Joanna Bobin

Joanne Henry

John Mackay

Jonathan Bailey

Jonathan Jude

Jordan Alexandra

Joseph Akubeze

Joseph MacNab

Julian Ovenden

Julie Andrews

Kaja Chan

Karlina Grace-Paseda

Kathryn Drysdale

Kush Mukerji

Leah Brotherhead

Leo Wan

Letty Thomas

Liam Noble

Liam Woon

Lorn MacDonald

Lorraine Ashbourne

Louis Cunningham

Louis Gaunt

Lucas Booth-Clibborn

Lucinda Raikes

Lucy Vandi

Luke Newton

Luke Pierre

Luke Thompson

Lynette Clarke

Mark Ramsey

Martins Imhangbe

Matthew Carter

Matthew Cottle

Melissa Advani

Michael Culkin

Michael Magnet

Michael Spicer

Mike Sengelow

Molly McGlynn

Naomi Preston-Low

Nathan Vidal

Ned Porteous

Neil Smye

Nicholas Shaw

Nicola Coughlan

Nikkita Chadha

Oli Higginson

Olivia Barrowclough

Olivia Suggett

Oscar Coleman

Oscar Porter

Paul G. Raymond

Paul Herzberg

Paul Hunter

Phil Snowden

Phoebe Dynevor

Pippa Haywood

Pippa Rathborne

Polly Walker

Priya Kansara

Ram Gupta

Raul Fernandes

Ray Macallan

Regé-Jean Page

Richard Pepple

Richard Stirling

Rob Kendrick

Robert Wilfort

Ross Cullum

Ruby Barker

Ruby Stokes

Rupert Evans

Rupert Vansittart

Rupert Young

Ruth Gemmell

Sabrina Bartlett

Sam Frenchum

Sam Haygarth

Sam Meakin

Sandra Teles

Sarah Junillon

Sarah Lawn

Seren Benbow-Hart

Shelley Conn

Sherise Blackman

Shobu Kapoor

Simon Lennon

Simon Ludders

Simone Ashley

Steph Lacey

Stephen Patten

Stuart Organ

Sukh Ojla

Tedroy Newell

Terri Ann Bobb-Baxter

Theresa Godly

Thomas Flynn

Tom Christian

Tom Lorcan

Tom Mannion

Tom Milligan

Tosh Wanogho-Maud

Vincent Davies

Will Tilston

Crew

Aaron Shiels
Abbigail Richards
Abby McDonald
Abi Monck
Abigail Adeosun
Adam Chard
Adam James Phillips
Adam Smith
Adam Vines
Adem Aydin
Adrian Monroy Diaz
Adrian Wright
Adriene Whitwell
Aella Jordan Edge
Aeneas McDonald
Agust Baldursson
AJ Prior
Akhil John
Akiya McKnight
Alain Bety
Alan Emanuel
Aldo Rosati
Alec McIlvaney
Alex Clements
Alex Conway
Alex Davis
Alex Drewett
Alex Gordon
Alex Smith
Alex Streeter
Alexander Breitfeld
Alexander Hale
Alexandra Drescher
Alexandra Kessie
Alexandra Patsavas
Alexis O'Brien
Aleysha Minns
Alfie Carusone
Alfie Hobden
Ali Griffiths
Alice Cridland
Alice Driscoll
Alice Godfrey
Alice Man
Alice Shilling
Alice Smart
Alicia Hood
Alison Baker
Alison Beard
Alison Eakle
Alison Gartshore
Alison Griffiths
Alison Jones
Aliveena Darr
Alix Milan

Alrick Riley
Amazing Space
Amber Frisenda
Amy Mansfield
Amy Martin
Amy McIntyre
Ana Baltova-Vercuiel
Anders Dick
Andi Coldwell
Andrea Hathazi
Andréa Loy
Andrea Williams
Andreas Ayling
Andreas Feix
Andrew Burford
Andrew Eadie
Andrew Hellesen
Andrew Hobbs
Andrew Mash
Andrew Share
Andy Dixon
Andy Gizzarelli
Andy Good
Andy Short
Angelo Palazzo
Aniruddha Satam
Anissa Senoussi
Anita Berkhane
Anna Chandler
Anna Gieniusz
Annabelle Hood
Anne Mouli Castillo
Anne-Marie Kanani
Annette Malone
Annie Laks
Anthony Cupples
Anthony McCartan
Antoine Molenat
Anton Badstuber
Antoni Kujawa
Antonio Rodriguez Diaz
April Nash
Archie Lodewyke
Arron Glover
Arthur Shepherd
Ashlee Sutherland
Ashley Fosbrook
Asia Paletskaya
Aurelien Lemonnier
Ava Milne
Avji Delega
Axel Gillot
Aynee Osborn
Barbara Hauser
Barbara Ohren

Barnaby Boulton
Beau Brett
Becca Wolfe
Beck Selmes
Becky Garrity
Becky Marks
Bella Quinn
Ben Ashmore
Ben Holt
Ben Johnston
Ben Okpu
Ben Pettie
Ben White
Benjamin Grisel
Benjamin Jean
Benjamin Mitnick
Benjamin Tron
Bernie O'Brian
Berto Zavala
Beth Deluce
Beth Long
Beth Marshall
Beth Parry
Betsy Beers
Bilal El Harrak
Billy Hancox
Billy Pidgley
Billy Quinn AMPS
Billy Stockwell
Billy West
Birgit "Bebe" Dierken
Bran Hopkins
Brandon Evans
Brandon Jones
Brandon Wilson
Brett Parnham
Brian Chandler
Brian Nickels
Brian Zwiener
Bridget Case
Bridget Durnford
Brittany DuBay
Bronwyn Yardie
Brooke Hodges
Brooke McGowan
Bruce Newton
Bryan Biermann
Bryony Satchell
Callum Clements
Callum Hodgkinson
Callum Martin
Cameron Frankley
Cameron Hobbs
Camilla Botterell-Race
Camille Evans

Camille Poiriez
Carina Kill
Carlos Fontanarrosa
Carlos Garcia Barragan
Carly Griffith
Carly Mills
Carole Prentice
Carolin Pech
Caroline Barton
Caroline Dreesman
Carolyn Corben
Caron Newman
Carrie Turner
Castle Howard Estate
Caterina da Via
Caterina Falce
Catharina Eden
Catherine Francis-
    Driscoll
Catherine Mullan
Catrin Atkinson
Catriona Bradley
Cavin Dempsey
Cavin John Dempsey
Celeste Harper Davis
Céline Pourcelot
Ceylan Shevket Jawara
Chan Chi Wan
Char Dent
Charles Havord
Charlie Bennett
Charlie Doe
Charlie Doult
Charlie Oldfield
Charlotte Allen
Charlotte Armstrong
Charlotte Curtis
Charlotte Dent
Charlotte Gooding
Charlotte Morrison
Charlotte Scott-Gray
Cheryl Dunye
Chi Lewis Parry
Chloe Waugh
Chris Barnett
Chris Dickinson
Chris Donovan
Chris Gill
Chris Hankey
Chris Poullay
Chris Sweeney
Chris Van Dusen
Christophe Jeudy
Christopher Gaikwad
Christopher Louca

Claire Higgins
Claire Matthews
Claudio Monk
Cliff Lim
Cody Relf
Cole Edwards
Colin Eade
Colin Gallagher
Connor Hagerty
Craig Dowson
Craig Elderfield
Craig Holbrook
Craig Sparkes
Curtis Burrell
Cyrielle Bounser
Daisy Hodgkinson
Dan Carter
Dan Huntley
Dan Riordan
Danee Rose
Daniel Cairns
Daniel Goodall
Daniel James Grove
Daniel Marlow
Daniel Robinson
Daniel Woodard
Daniele La Mura
Danielle Johnally
Danielle Millington
    Peck
Danny Brown
Danny Edwards
Daria Aksiuta
Darius Bradbear-Brown
Darrell Briggs
Darren 'Basil' Johnson
Darren Baba
Darren Burgess
Darren Hayward
Darren Haywood
Dasha Aksyuta
Dave Bell
Dave Blinko
Dave Clayton
Dave Dobson
Dave Rankin
David Addison Myers
David Bell
David Crewdson
David Hartnett
David Myers
David Olusoga
David Palm
David Riley
David S. Di Pietro

David Stafford
David Verity
Davide D'Antonio
Dean Blyth
Dean Burtenshaw
Deb Adair
Deborah Tallentire
Dee Koppang O'Leary
Denise Chan
Dianah Jane Coleman
Dianne St. James
Dom Anthony
Dominic Devine
Dominic Preece
Dominic Seal
Dominic Wilson
Dorney Court
Doug Perfili
Dougie Hawkes
Drew Marsden
Dwight Carter
Dylan Howell
Dylan Newton
Dylan Saville
Eba Tahmina Islame
Eboni Price
Edward Farmer
Edwina Mitrica
Eleanor Robinson
Elena Dimcheva
Elhein De Wet
Elisabet Berggren
Elizabeth Benjamin
Elizabeth King
Elizabeth Talbot
Ellen Erikson
Ellen Mirojnick
Ellie Muscutt
Elliot Smith
Elliott Meddings
Els Ariadne Wentink
Emanuela Borruso
Emily Beatty
Emily Brazier
Emily Burling
Emily Lancaster
Emily Lowe
Emily Perry
Emily Prieditis
Emily Radakovic
Emma Bedwell
Emma Davis
Emma Devonald
Emma Harrison
Emma Howarth

Emma Pelliciari	Gert Van Dermeersch	Ivy Briones	John Clarke	Kelly Smith	Linda Baker
Emma Rigby	Giles Greenwood	Ivy Hegelheimer	John Dalton	Kelsey Barry	Lionel Garrote
Emma Taylor-Gilli	Gillian Martins	Ivy Sarreal	John Dew	Kelsey Hare	Lisa Peardon
Emma Woodcock	Gilly Martin	Jack Clark	John Duggan	Kelvin Richard	Lisa Pope
Emmanuel Humbert	Gina Cromwell	Jack Knott	John Glaser	Kenny Crouch	Liz Khan-Greig
Endre Balint	Gina Lewis	Jack Murphy	John Kolthammer	Kerry Matthews	Lizzie King
English Heritage	Giovanni Facci	Jack Wren	John May	Kevin Biggs	Lois Gration
Eniko Karadi	Giulio Petralia	Jacob Fortgang	John Mcmeekin	Kevin Jones	Lorenzo Mancianti
Enric Ortuno	Graeme Eglin	Jacob Worthington	John Mullan	Kevin Kilmister	Lorna Cook
Erika Okvist	Graham Samels	Jade Robertson	John Norster	Kevin Moore	Lorraine Cooksley
Erin Cancino	Greg Evans	Jake Bush	John Piggott	Kevin Plumb	Lottie Forrester
Esme Coleman	Greg Howard	Jake Kensley	John Ray	Kevin Pratten-Stone	Lou Bannell
Etienne Newton	Greg Keith	James Borne	John Rook	Kevin Woodhouse	Lou-Lou Igbokwe
Euan Coe	Greg Powell	James Evered	John W. Glaser III	Kevin Young	Louis Falcon
Eugene Rachevsky	Gregory Fox	James Lay	John Whickman	Kez Keyte	Louise Graham
Eva Mills	Gregory T. Evans	James Pavey	John Willson	Khalid Shafique	Louise Mackay
Faith Johnston	Grytė Navardauskaitė	James White	Johnny White	Kirsa Ferreiro	Louise Rashman
Farida Ghwedar	Gsus López	Jamie Calvert	Jon Beacham	Dominguez	Louise Sargeant
Farrah Yip	Guglielmo Emmolo	Jamie Davies Evans	Jon Boylan	Kirsti Reid	Lucy Benson
Federico Righi	Guillaume Ménard	Jamie Karitzis	Jon Cadwell	Kirstie Robinson	Lucy Denny
Fiona Davis	Guy Tsujimoto	Jamie Lamb	Jon Harvy Santos	Kirsty McKirdy	Lucy Hassan
Fiona Lobo Cranston	Hailu Ashaw	Jamie Shelley	Jonas Mondua	Kitty Whately	Lucy May Green
Fiona Murkin	Hannah Brooks	Jane Bedden	Jonathan Arias	Kris Bowers	Lucy Rowley
Flora Christian	Hannah Greig	Jane Bogunovic	Jonathan Igla	Kristian Raciti	Ludo Frege
Flora Moyes	Hannah Miller-Burton	Jane Karen	Jordan Carter	Kyran Bishop	Luis Ormeño Fernández
Fran Conte	Hannah Page	Janet Lin	Josh Crisp	Lara Prentice	Luka Traynor Jones
Fran Ponisi	Hannah Rowe	Jasmine O'Gilvie	Josh Curtis	Laura Frecon	Luke Anstiss
Francesca Casilli	Hannah Segal	Jasmine Wong	Josh Dempsey	Laura Murphy	Luke Daniels
Francesca Guzzetta	Hannah Smith	Jason Relf	Josh Kadish	Laura Sim	Luke Farley
Francesca Piergiovanni	Harjit Chaggar	Jason Walker	Josh Shelley	Laura Sindall	Lyn Elizabeth Paolo
Francesco Antonio	Harry Elvidge	Javier Gonzalez	Joshua Beattie	Laura Wright	Lynda J Pearce
Maggi	Harry Foster	Jay Ross	Joshua Dempsey	Lauren Kilcar	Lynne Mattingley
Francis Campbell	Harry Gay	Jaz Blair-Edmund	Joshua Faulkner	Lauren Newberry	Magda Sobolewska
Franzisca Masia	Harry Good	Jean Ash	Joshua Okpala	Lauren Wilkinson	Maia Herzog-Lee
Freddie Gollins	Harry Landymore	Jean Kelly	Josie Fergusson	Laurens Vermeulen	Maja Milisavljevic
Fry Martin	Harry Pepper	Jed Sheahan	Joy C. Mitchell	Laurent Arnaud	Malika Ruzmetova
Gabriel Bujita	Hasan Khan	Jeffrey Jur	Joy Mitchell	Leanne Danielle	Marc Pilcher
Gabriel Hernandez	Hattie McGill	Jeffrey St. Louis	Juan Tudela	Goymer	Marc Ridley
Gabrielle Firth	Haydn Webb	Jen Seip	Julia Quinn	Lebo "Boo" Motjuoadi	Marcelo Aprile
Garth Sewell	Heather Varley	Jenna McGowan	Julian Smith	Lee Dilley	Marcelo Payes
Gary DeLeone	Heidi Ashton	Jenna Miller	Julie Anne Robinson	Lee Grego	Marco Esquivel
Gary Donoghue	Hélder Tomás	Jennifer Addo	Julie Goodchild	Lee Kenny	Marco Masotti
Gary Handley	Helen Beasley	Jenny Gauci	Junel Ali	Leigh Court	Marcus Ward
Gary Lasson	Helen Christie	Jenny Rhodes-McLean	Justin Kamps	Leigh Tempany-Boon	Margarethe Schmoll
Gary McKay	Helen Rootkin	Jess Averbeck	Kamanza Amihyia	Leigh Woolf	Margie Fortune
Gary Page	Helena Jung	Jess Brownell	Karen Foote	Leila Cohan-Miccio	Maria Endara
Gary Walter	Hilary Holdsworth	Jess Corley	Karl Hui	Leo Bund	Maria Gomez
Ged Henshaw	Hilary Mills	Jess Phillips	Karolyn Reece	Leo Osborne	Maria Heather Dockrill
Geetika Tandon Lizardi	Holden Chang	Jesse Ehredt	Kasia Najdek	Les Jones	Mariana Pitonakova
Gemma Sealey	Hollie Williams	Jessica Davis	Kasia Rymar	Lesley & Mike at Pickled	Mark Erksine
Gene D'Cruze	Honor Roche	Jessica Lennox	Kat Blair	Greens	Mark Holmes
Geoffrey Slack	Humphrey Bangham	Jessie Deol	Kate Ellison	Lewis Barringer	Mark Horner
George Day	Hyson Pereira	Jillian Apel	Kate Laver	Lewis Peake	Mark MacRae
George Harrison	Ian Griffin	Jo Barker	Katharine Phillips	Lewis Sanders	Mark Molnar
George Jenkins	Ian Tansley	Jo Deluce	Katherine Mellville	Lewis Westing	Mark Nutkins
George Kalimerakis	Ian Woolf	Joanna Barton	Katie Aldous	Liam Clements	Mark O'Shea
George Makhshigian	Ibrahim Ajala	Joanna Osborn	Katie Harlow	Liam Coffey	Mark Rafferty
George Sayer	Imogen Murray	Jodie Bell	Katie McClung	Liam Daniel	Mark Rudd
Georgia Hobbs	Ingenuity Studios	Joe Baker	Katie Noriega	Liam Doran	Mark Sneddon
Georgia Hume	Ingrid Polakovicova	Joe Blunt	Katrina Reschke	Liam Linbonton	Mark Webb
Georgina Musgrave	Inka Polakovicova	Joe Hissey	Kaye Woodcock	Liam McDonnell	Mark Wynne-Pedder
Georgina Sparrow	Isabelle Cook	Johann Cruikshank	Kayleigh Sims	Lidija Skorucak	Marketa Hrusecka
Geraldine O'Connell	Iva Quint	John Boylan	Kelly Phillips	Lilly Hanbury	Martin Cox

Martin Duffy
Martin McDonald
Martin McShane
Mathew Finnigan
Matilda Musto
Matt Craufurd
Matt Crook
Matt Jackson
Matt Markham
Matt Pevic
Matthew d'Angibau
Matthew Finnigan
Matthew Kay
Matthew T. Lynn
Mausum Rathod
Max Hatfield
Max Mason
Max McLay
Max Wrightson
Maxence Delaforge
Maxim Condon
Maxime Pillonel
Maya Ayele
Mayank Modi
Mayowa Abi Adeosun
Mazin Mohammed
Mazz Cummings
Meghan O'Connell
Melanie Geley
Melissa Rogula
Melody Hood
Mia Hope Radford
Mia Stewart
Micah Hazzard
Michael Birch
Michael Boden
Michael Harkin
Michael Hastead
Michael Mungroo
Michael Papal
Michael Weaver
Michaela Miesen
Micheal Boden
Michela Marini
Michelle Buck
Michelle Wright
Mick Clark
Mick Hurrell
Mick Lord
Mickey Rixon
Mike Light
Mike Pain
Milly Barter
Minal Mistry
Miriam Pavese
Mitchell Brown
Mitchell Kohen
Mohamed Wazeem
Afzal
Mollie Barr
Momoco
Monty Till
Morgane Herbstmeyer

Mr. Peter and
Mrs. Melissa
O'Sullivan
Murray Aston
Myles Wynne-Pedder
Nacho Thomas
Nadya Ivanova
Nancy Bray
Nancy Thompson
Natalie Brown
Natalie Papageorgiadis
Natalie Segal
Natasha Anderson
Natasha McMahon
Natasha Reynell
Natasha Webb
Nathan Twitchett
Naz Amin
Neil Cairns
Neil Glynn
Neil Mulholland
Neil Samels
Nell Robinson
Niall Oglivy
Niamh Cunningham
Nic Turton
Nicholas Cruz
Nicholas Snookes
Nick Edwards
Nick Parsons
Nicki Ballantyne
Nicky Demuth
Nicky Sandford
Nicolas Gresland
Nicole Whittle
Nicolo Ciprian
Nieves Allen
Nigel Crisp
Nikki Demetriou
Nile Hylton
Noel Cowell
Noelle Arias
North Mymms Park
Oliver Goldstick
Oliver Hughes
Oliver Poole
Oliver Stotter
Oliver Whickman
Olivia Ashman
Olivia Boix De La Cruz
Olivia Evelyn Bond
Olivia Grimmer
Painshill Park
Pamela Ip
Pankaj Bajpai
Pascha Hanaway
Patricia Lucia Locche
Paul Cowell
Paul Deluce
Paul Farrington
Paul Fullerton
Paul Lee
Paul Tomlinson

Paulo Mateus
Pearl Haslam
Penny Taylor
Petar Petrov
Peter 'Skip' Howard
Peter Alberti
Peter Brown
Peter Hodges
Peter Philip Clarke
Peter Quinn
Peter Rotter
Peter Yip
Phil Aichinger
Phil Stander
Phil The Bowser
Phil Wong
Philip Ball
Philipp Blaubach
Philippa Long
Phuong Thai
Picture Shop
Pierre Charles
Pilar Seijo
Poonam Thanki
Priya Atwal
Quinn Boyd
Rachael Jones
Rachel Garlick
Rachel Neill
Rachel Pedder
Rachel Penfold
Rachel Welford
Rae Benjamin
Rajiv Bedi
Ralitsa Karova
Ramin Adilov
Rashid Phoenix
Raven Tahzib
Ray Ingardfield
Ray Relf
Rebecca Wolfe
Rene Karp
Rich Harris
Richard Grant
Richard Moss
Richard Potter
Richard Rogan
Rick Larson
Rikki Clarke
Rimanie Bratley
Rob McGregor
Rob Portus
Rob Stapleton
Robb Raufus
Robbie Chance
Robert Dixey
Robert Lillie
Robert McGregor
Robin (Bobby) Soutar
Robin Ashworth-Cape
Robyn Girvan
Romain Couturiaux
Ronan Carr

Rosa Diamond
Rosie Wessels
Rowan Pierce
Rupert Davies
Ruth Mongey
Ruth Young
Ruxandra Cristoiu
Ryan Garrad
Ryan McCarthy
Ryan Monteith
Ryan Welsh
Ryan Wheeler
Sadie Tilbury
Saffron Bramley-Astle
Sahil Jindal
Sally Llewellyn
Saloum N'jie
Sam Brooke-Taylor
Sam Burbridge
Sam Dent
Sam Jones
Sam Killingback
Sam Knox-Johnston
Sam Parnell
Sam Pickering
Samuel Jackson
Sanaz Missaghian
Sandie Bailey
Sara Austin
Sara Fischer
Sara Krantz
Sara Kuna
Sarada McDermott
Sarah Bridge
Sarah Croft
Sarah Dollard
Sarah Glenn
Sarah Howson
Sarah Jane Mills
Sarah L. Thompson
Sarah Lyall
Sarah Tapscott
Sarah Turner
Sasha Amani
Sasha Bowen
Sasha Imani
Sataish O'Shea
Saurav Ojha
Scarlet Shay
Scott Allen
Scott Collins
Scott Peters
Seamus Shanley
Sean "Jack" Murphy
Sean Duffy
Sebastian Olmos
Olivares
Sedi Kukwikila
Shahin Moatazed-
Keyvany
Shaniqua Y. Rivers
Shannon Funston Coker
Shannon O'Hara

Sharon Mansfield
Shaun Steer
Shawn Broes
Shawn Dixon
Sheralee Hamer
Sheree Folkson
Sherise Blackman
Shevaun Wood
Shonda Rhimes
Sidney Cosse
Sidonie Nicholson
Sim Camps
Simon Fraser
Simon Gill
Simon Lane
Sofian Francis
Solveig Ferlet
Sophie Brown
Sophie Canale
Sophie James Frost
Sophie Lambe
Sophie Lyell
Sophie Pyecoroft
Stefan Petcu
Stefano Bagnoli
Stephen Enticott
Stephen Fitzmaurice
Stephen Kaye
Stephen Wall
Stephen Williams
Steve "Barney" Barnett
Steve Bream
Steve Broadfoot
Steve Clarke
Steve Dent
Steve Fitzpatrick
Steve Fox
Steve Lewis
Steve Paciello
Steve Rogers
Steven Reeves
Stuart Piddington-Wall
Stuart Sinclair
Students of
Boomsatsuma
Sue Bradbear
Suman Pal
Susan Reed
Susanna Hurrell
Susie Coleridge-Smith
Sven Müller
Tamsin Balcanquall
Tania Couper
Tara Keenan
Tasmin Balcanquall
Ted Leaning
Temilolu Babasanya
Terry Bamber
Tesa Kubicek
Tessa Gibson
Theo Spearman
Thomas Ball
Thomas Bassett

Thomas Batten
Thomas Gordon
Thomas J. Bronson
Thomas Lane
Thomas Lemaille
Thomas Prothero
Tiffany Hall
Tim Blackwood
Tim Perkins
Tim Surrey
Tim Woodcock
Timothy James Leask
TJ Singh
Tom "Ozzie" Osborne
Tom Bassett
Tom Bull
Tom Cowlishaw
Tom Davey
Tom Gordon
Tom Hussey
Tom Lock
Tom Locke
Tom Maguire
Tom Osborne
Tom Smith
Tom van Dop
Tom Verica
Tony Cooper
Tony Dawson
Tony Hood
Tony O'Callaghan
Tracy Stiles
Trethanna Trevarthen
Trevor Brooks
Tricia Brock
Ulrika Akander
Valerie Aragon
Valerie Cheung
Vanessa Brogna
Victor Tomi
Victoria Olamide
Johnson
Vojta Stanek
Vonnie Meyrick-Brook
Waqqas Sheikh
Warren Deluce
Wayne Fitzsimmons
Westwind Media
Will Anderson
Will Hughes-Jones
William Correia
William Jensen
Williams Skeels
Xavier Lake
Yanika Waters
Zach Du Toit
Ziggy Gray
Zoe Brown
Zoe Geddes

MARYSUE
RUCCI
BOOKS
SCRIBNER

Marysue Rucci Books/Scribner
An Imprint of Simon & Schuster, Inc.
1230 Avenue of the Americas
New York, NY 10020

First Marysue Rucci Books/Scribner hardcover edition October 2022

MARYSUE RUCCI BOOKS and colophon are trademarks of Simon & Schuster, Inc.

SCRIBNER and colophon are trademarks of The Gale Group, Inc., used under license by Simon & Schuster, Inc.

For information about special discounts for bulk purchases, please contact Simon & Schuster Special Sales at 1-866-506-1949 or business@simonandschuster.com.

The Simon & Schuster Speakers Bureau can bring authors to your live event. For more information or to book an event, contact the Simon & Schuster Speakers Bureau at 1-866-248-3049 or visit our website at www.simonspeakers.com.

Interior design by Insight Editions

Manufactured in the United States of America

10 9 8 7 6 5 4 3 2 1

Library of Congress Cataloging-in-Publication Data has been applied for.

ISBN 978-1-6680-0107-3
ISBN 978-1-6680-0108-0 (ebook)

Unit photography courtesy Netflix/Liam Daniel

Interviews with Erika Okvist on p. 214 and p. 216 adapted from articles in *Glamour* (March 25, 2022) and *Marie Claire* (March 29, 2022). Interview with Sophie Canale on p. 177 adapted from an article in *Harper's Bazaar* (March 23, 2022).

...ing more exhilarating than taking a gamble...

...with nothing but regret. Of course...

...now that nothing is more exciting than...

...lers have... only show... Which leaves gossip in short supply...

...ation. So we shall all have to sit back and wait for them to show their hand...

...able of permanent black ink. Gambling for Gossip? It is worthy of note that...

...newlyweds are no doubt still secluded in nuptial bliss. We could expect the...

arrival within the year. They are the perfect couple and have both survived the...

holds for them and how they emerge from their post-nuptial bubble, ready to often...

have seen the latest art exhibition brought to us all by Mr. Clytherland. We...

last few years as he is often away travelling and finding so-called 'inspiration'...

his inspiration slightly closer to home. I believe this is the largest. This could...

be a reason. So this is my conclusion... Of course an artist needs his muse, but...

Meaning that one must be very careful if one is to become a muse as they could...

lifetime of scandal. For the more observant of my readers who have attended the...

strong resemblance to one of our newer townsfolk. Of course this may just be a...

the exhibition. Perhaps this is in case she is caught too close to one of the figure...

lady is happily married, or so we thought. Perhaps things are not as they seem...

country to visit her sister. So sadly she shall not get to witness the wonderful...